The ART of
TRANSFORMATION

The **ART** of **TRANSFORMATION**

Three Things Churches Do
That Change **EVERYTHING**

PAUL FROMBERG

Church Publishing
NEW YORK

Unless otherwise noted, the Scripture quotations contained herein are from the New Revised Standard Version Bible, copyright © 1989 by the Division of Christian Education of the National Council of Churches of Christ in the U.S.A. Used by permission. All rights reserved.

Scripture quotations marked NJB are from *The New Jerusalem Bible*, copyright © 1985 by Darton, Longman & Todd, Ltd. and Doubleday, a division of Random House, Inc. Reprinted by Permission.

Church Publishing
19 East 34th Street
New York, NY 10016
www.churchpublishing.org

Cover design by Jennifer Kopec, 2Pug Design
Typeset by Denise Hoff

Library of Congress Cataloging-in-Publication Data

Names: Fromberg, Paul, author.
Title: The art of transformation : three things churches do that
    change everything / Paul Fromberg.
Description: New York : Church Publishing, 2017.
Identifiers: LCCN 2016054478 (print) | LCCN 2017011167 (ebook)
    | ISBN 9780819233752 (ebook) | ISBN 9780819233745 (pbk.)
Subjects: LCSH: Church renewal. | Change--Religious aspects--Christianity.
Classification: LCC BV600.3 (ebook) | LCC BV600.3 .F755 2017 (print)
    | DDC 253--dc23
LC record available at https://lccn.loc.gov/2016054478

Contents

For the people of St. Gregory's Church
and my friend Sara Miles,
all of whom show me the image
of the invisible God

Introduction:
Why Transformation?

Church is different. It's distinct.
It's hard to put into words
how it's different. It's not business.
It's not school. It's not neighbors.
It's a different kind of chosen
relationship with people.

—*Janet T.*

O N THE SURFACE, transformation seems straightforward: you decide that you want to see a change in your life, and you make change happen. But the phenomenon of transformation is complex and goes to the heart of what it means to be whole and to live in a way that makes more of the life God gives us. Transformation is a discipline, like training for a marathon. Transformation is an art, like practicing calligraphy. Transformation is a process, like cultivating relationships with people we love. Transformation doesn't happen overnight; it takes time. It is a discipline that communities and individuals must accept consciously. And transformation has the power to change everything about people's lives and the congregations that they comprise.

The art of transformation is about people's behavior, which means that those who seek it have to change the way that they live. Transformation involves giving up what we know for the sake of what we don't know. It means giving up a certain amount of control in our lives. It takes the kind of personal examination that requires time and vulnerability. Transformation takes courage; it requires a willingness to share your life, passions, and struggles with other people. It means living authentically with people, not as an exception, but as a normal part of life. Transformation is something more than change; it must happen in relationship to others. You can change some parts of yourself on your own, but transformation requires you to share your life with another, to trust them with what is happening in the deepest parts of your experience. The art of transformation takes all of our attention, all of our passion, and all of our love. Despite these challenges, people continue to strive for transformation. This book is my best attempt at describing the art of transformation, and how it works in people's lives, particularly in the context of congregational life.

I can still remember the moment that I gave up on my fear of change and began to say "yes" to God's call to transformation. It was a soft, dark night in Southern California—one of those few moments when the darkness seemed to win out over the burning lights of the city. I had just stepped out of All Saints Episcopal Church in Pasadena into the courtyard at the center of the magnificent building that houses that congregation. I was a student at Fuller Theological Seminary, a large, Evangelical graduate school where I was studying marriage and family therapy. Although I was raised in the conservative Church of Christ and had flirted with denominations from Roman Catholicism to Pentecostalism, my heart was settling in the Episcopal Church. I decided that attending the adult confirmation class would be a good addition to my education about the church; I never suspected that the class would undo the man I had been and invite a new creation. What I heard gave me a sense that going to church was about more than just trying to be good; going to church was about beauty and justice and looking beyond pat answers to deep mysteries that satisfied me in ways that certitude never did. In the darkness of that night, I realized that I was in the midst of a huge transformation in my life.

I was looking for a way out of the spiritual bind that had paralyzed me. I was never going to be able to pull off ministry in the Church of Christ or the Evangelical movement of the mid-1980s. Although I kept trying to ignore the fact, I knew deep in my bones that I was gay, and it wasn't just a phase I was going through or a bad habit I might overcome; being gay was who I was, and that wasn't something that my conservative church could help me live into. Even deeper down I knew that being gay wasn't just something that had happened to me. I was beginning to realize that being gay was God's gift to me. The Episcopal Church seemed like a place that would never leave me and that I would never have to abandon. In a moment, on a dark fall night, I received God's call not just to leave my cradle denomination, but to grow into God's call to be gay, and to become a priest in the Episcopal Church. Four years later, I realized that call and was ordained.

I worked at a large church for nearly ten years, before I began to realize that something was wrong. On the surface, everything was fine. I learned the art of priest-craft well. I learned the right way to do my work with church people. I was successful. I earned responsibility and was admired by my colleagues. Despite all of this, I found myself in the same kind of spiritual bind I'd experienced when I was first called to transformation. The work was beginning to feel automatic. My favorite part of worship became the dismissal. I performed my role as a priest well, but there was something missing; there was something more I wanted in my love affair with God.

When I realized that I had to go deeper into the mystery of my life in God, it was another call to transformation. Working in the church was good, but it was predictable. As much as I preached about grace and repentance and love, it seemed like change came slowly if change came at all. My greatest fear was that I would have to either walk away from the Church or put my head down and numb my way through a career in ministry. A couple of years before this I'd confided my despair to a friend who said, "Most of us get to where you are sooner or later; you just got there sooner." The kind of cynical detachment that was growing in me was draining me of the surge I had felt when I first said "yes" to God.

It was at this moment of desperation in my life that I began to learn more about the power of transformation. It began in 1997, the first time that I walked into St. Gregory of Nyssa Episcopal Church in San Francisco. What I discovered at St. Gregory's was something that I had only hoped was possible: a community of people who cared more about doing things "well" than doing them "right."

St. Gregory's has always been a community of transformation. Richard Fabian and Donald Schell founded St. Gregory's in 1978. Their hope was to create an intentionally experimental congregation. They didn't care as much about the way that their denomination told them to be as they cared about the way that communities actually worked. Rick and Donald began to imagine a church where the liturgy—the people's life in worship—would form the community. They described a congregation that would take risks, learn from failures, reinvent traditional practices, and trust that God was at work in the whole thing. They founded a community rooted in the gift of God's grace to people of all faiths—or no faith at all. They claimed that everyone was God's friend, without exception; people are made friends of God by the loving service of Christ. Friendship with God comes freely; it comes as an expression of the eternal love that is God the Holy Trinity, and it comes with an expectation that human lives will be transformed by God's love.

In 2004, I began a new ministry at St. Gregory's, one that eventually resulted in my being called as the congregation's leader in 2008. From the moment I first encountered St. Gregory's, to the day I was called to be its rector, to my doctoral study in the phenomenon of transformation, to the day I sat down to write this book, the people who make this remarkable church have challenged me to change in unexpected, beautiful ways. They have taught me the value of striving for transformation. The fact that St. Gregory's is an Episcopal Church is, for the most part, irrelevant to the lessons I've learned about the art of transformation. The Episcopal Church is my tribe, but I'm convinced that the kind of transformation I've experienced at St. Gregory's can happen in any denomination.

In 2011, I began to study transformation as a part of my doctoral work. I approached the question of transformation within the context of my congregation, St. Gregory's, wanting to find out what we were doing that made a difference in the lives of our members. My research was based on an academic study of the phenomenon of transformation as well as individual interviews with a cross-section of the congregation.

The academic literature showed me that there are many methods and modalities that influence transformation in people's lives. Three influences emerged in the interviews that I held with members of St. Gregory's: aesthetic experience, social engagement, and friendship. The category of aesthetic experience included people's experiences of worship, music, art, and poetry. People's experience of social engagement included direct action in the community outside the congregation, public advocacy for political change, and working to make justice a reality in disenfranchised people's lives. Friendship was an experience that people mentioned in every interview; it included both relationships based on shared affinity as well as finding friendship with strangers. The people of St. Gregory's appreciate that they are stakeholders and are accustomed to having real authority regarding the course of the congregation's life. We share a history of working for growth and transformation in our shared life. All of this made St. Gregory's an ideal setting within which to learn more about the phenomenon of transformation and the factors that influence it.

Transformation takes place at St. Gregory's on the basis of what we do day by day as a community. "Making church together" is the way that we talk about this work of being a community. When we make church together, it always centers on three practices: welcoming beauty, engaging in social action, and living in friendship. As I studied St. Gregory's, I found that these three practices form the foundation for everything the community does. Our practices of beauty, action, and friendship take place in the context of the extravagant welcome extended to everyone who walks through our doors. We welcome everyone in the same way that Jesus does in the Gospels: openly, without any expectation, including the expectation that any achievement is required of you before receiving what God has in store. Our story, the gospel story, says that God is freely giving to everyone. What we receive from God is for us to use to create something new for the world.

In a real sense, St. Gregory's is a community of amateurs. You don't have to be accomplished to have a creative stake in the community: this is a place where people can experiment and test out new ways of approaching worship, learning, relationships, and the work God is putting before them.

It is important to remember that the art of transformation is not something that is reserved for Episcopalians. If anything, the opposite is the case; Episcopalians are not called "God's Chosen Frozen" for no reason. So, the energy that comes from creatively engaging the way church is made is something outside the wheelhouse of many Episcopal churches. What matters more than a particular denomination is a congregation where people are all in, ready to risk everything, fall flat on their faces, pick themselves up, and see what they've learned in the process. Transformation calls everyone to look beyond the way that things have always been done to see a new creation. Transformation is an art that any denomination can practice: it will work for Methodists, or Roman Catholics, or Unitarians, or any spiritual community that is willing to take risks.

There are no insiders and no outsiders when it comes to transformation: everyone gets to participate. Transformation isn't about character or good genes. All that transformation requires is showing up and taking action in the context of community. This is why transformation is a phenomenon that can thrive in congregations. The practices of beauty, action, and friendship are what many congregations strive to do already. But to exercise these practices and realize transformation, congregations must recognize three things:

- Transformation takes time: it requires self-reflection and a willingness to be open to new perspectives on lived experiences.

- Transformation takes relationships: it requires a willingness to reflect on life experiences with other people and listen to their feedback.

- Transformation takes practice: we have to apply the new insights we discover and test them out in our lives.

Social scientists have studied the phenomenon of transformation since the late 1970s. The learning theorist Jack Mezirow first suggested the predictable way that transformation works in people's lives. It begins with a crisis or a changed situation in our lives. From this experience comes personal reflection as a result of facing the new reality. The process of transformation intensifies as people make new meanings out of previously held assumptions. Mezirow found that transformation needs both personal reflection and supportive, empathetic dialogue with other people who will recognize our emotions, perspectives, and sensitivities as we are changing.

One challenge that comes when we strive for transformation is that it requires people to become disciplined about sharing their stories with others. Maybe you've had the experience of deciding that your life needs to change. You may have become so fed up with the way things were that you began to look at the way things could be. So you began to make conscious choices to live in a new way. But you never talked about it with anyone else. You never confided in anyone your despair at the way things had always been in your life and your hope of change. You didn't talk to friends about your failures or triumphs along the way. You tried to do everything on your own. When that happens, your best attempts at change make only a short-term difference. If transformation is going to happen in your life, then you have to honestly share your life, your struggles, and your triumphs, with others.

Sharing your desire to change, the struggles you face, the joys you discover, makes you vulnerable to others. For many people, this is a difficult thing to do. You make a decision to change—maybe you even share the decision with a few people—but the risk of returning again and again to self-disclosure makes it easier to reply to those who ask how you're doing with a "just fine," or some other anodyne response. But the more you admit your own vulnerability, the greater the probability that you will experience real transformation in your life. Sharing your desire to change, and being consistent about sharing, results in a new perspective on your life, one that has the power to make you more accepting and more inclusive of others.

Another factor that empowers transformation is the degree to which you choose to do unfamiliar things and interact with unknown others. Trying out new practices, especially those that may seem scary or intimidating, strengthens people and gives us new perspective. Instead of seeing other people, and life in general, as threatening and fearful, you can begin to see yourself and others as bound in mutuality. Then, the things that had separated you from the other begin to blur and lose their meaning. Trying out new ways of being in the world is important to transformation because we create meaning in our lives out of lived experiences. When the ways that we've always done things stop working, when our current needs aren't met by old ways of doing things, when we feel like we're losing our way, we are ready for transformation. This way begins when we question old stories about our lives. These questions lead us to new insights. These insights guide our future actions. Then we begin to live our lives in new ways, acquiring new knowledge and skills. In order for it to be effective in your life, transformative practices must be lived out every day. Transformation is not just an intellectual process; it requires our emotions, experiences, relationships, and bodies. All of this results in recreated, abundant lives.

I believe that this process happens most profoundly in congregational life. People attend church for many reasons. But as the church becomes more of a social option than a social obligation, people attend church to find something they can't find anywhere else. As the ways we've always done church become less meaningful to people, it's important to ask what it is that congregations can do to connect people in deep, real ways. The fundamental fact is that people go to church to experience spiritual growth. You don't go to church to learn a set of doctrinal facts; you go because you want to see the beauty of God in the midst of community. The longing for something eternal, something beautiful, and something that connects disconnected lives invites transformation.

The problem is that the human longing for transformation may run into the congregation's desire to stay the same. More than one time I've heard some congregational leader say, "The seven last words of the church are, 'We've never done it that way before.'" It's a problem when social systems fear transformation, but even more challenging when church leaders block change because it threatens them personally. These places end up being completely resistant to change. Eventually, these kinds of congregations must choose between closing the doors permanently or risking everything for the sake of transformation. Congregations have to get used to stepping into the unknown, unmapped territory where God is at work. This is where the only thing that matters is our trust in God's care and catching the vision of the world that God holds for us. Stepping into the unknown challenges every congregation's commitment to *metanoia*: a new mind, reorientation, change, conversion of life—in other words, transformation.

Churches have the responsibility to teach transformation to their members; it is the church's primary purpose. And churches must teach this understanding that transformation is both attractive and challenging. My research has shown that most people who go to church are not opposed to change; they just don't know how to make it happen in their lives. Congregations come to know God as they work for transformation in the lives of their members. Every day that we struggle for transformation we learn to see God in new ways: active in the world, longing to draw the whole world in God's embrace.

Many changes have taken place in the years between the founding of St. Gregory's and this moment. However, the initial hope of creating an intentional community of transformation continues to be realized. All that we need is a desire to show up and a willingness to grow through the experience of what we do together. I've learned that what we do at St. Gregory's has the power to transform people's understanding of themselves as participants and leaders in the church. When people get to do real work in the church, it changes everything for them. People stop being passive consumers and become makers of church. More than this, the kind of growth that people experience is generative: it spreads from person to person and from the church to the world. Most important, St. Gregory's has taught me that church doesn't have to be boring, and people who work in the church don't have to be cynical. I've learned that the act of making church together will empower people to be powerful and wise and expand their vision of God, the world, and themselves.

In the following chapters, you will learn more about this remarkable church, its members, and what our experience teaches about the ways each of our lives can be changed by the art of transformation. We begin with beauty.

The Strange Necessity for Beauty

*The person who removes himself from
all hatred and fleshly odor and rises
above all low and earthbound things,
having ascended higher than the whole
earth in his aforementioned flight,
will find the only thing that is worth
longing for, and, having come close to
beauty, will become beautiful himself.*

—*Gregory of Nyssa*

I DIDN'T THINK ABOUT the dangers of creating a beautiful space for our Maundy Thursday service; I was simply delighting in making beauty with others, as we shared the work of dressing the church for Holy Week. What I remember is one of our heavy, metal, Ethiopian crosses, mounted on a stave, leaning against a wall. I recall moving the ladder into place to pull down supplies for the evening foot washing. What happened next was so quick: the ladder kicked the base of the cross, causing it to swing down like a scythe into my face. I hardly felt it when the cross hit me, but instinctively I pressed my palm against my right cheek. I turned to the tall mirror that hangs on the wall of the vestry, pulled my hand away, and saw a gaping wound less than an inch beneath my eye. "Stay calm. You have to lead the liturgy tonight," I said to myself as I walked to the tiny bathroom in the vestry. I pulled a wad of paper towels out of the dispenser and quickly pressed them against the wound.

I walked out of the vestry, as calmly as I could. About a half-dozen parishioners were busily working to transform the space around the altar into a dining room for our liturgy, spreading colorful tablecloths and arranging spring flowers. I found my coworker Sara Miles in the kitchen. "You need to drive me to the hospital; I think I need stitches." What I didn't say was, "Oh, and by the way, if the cross had been an inch taller I would have lost my eye." The thought filled me with nausea. Sara got behind the wheel of my car. I sat next to her, pressing my hand to my cheek, hoping that everything would get sewn up before the six o'clock service. I wanted the service to be beautiful. I wanted to keep making that beauty, and be there to see the cross that made me bleed, gleaming by the altar in the evening light. Talking non-stop to ease my anxiety I wise-cracked, "You have to suffer for beauty."

When we arrived at the emergency department, I stepped to the admission window where the charge nurse asked if mine was a workplace injury. "Not exactly. I mean—no. I was just getting ready for church." I phoned my husband, Grant, at his office and tried to explain what happened. "Are you okay?" What do you tell your beloved about a cross hitting you in the face and slashing it open during Holy Week? "I'll be fine." Later, Grant told me that his boss's response to the news was perfect San Francisco irony: "He got hit in the face with a cross? On Maundy Thursday? That's awesome!"

✄

Beauty animates us. The very first time I visited St. Gregory's was on a Saturday afternoon in 1997. I walked into the building, surprised to find it wide open, and was greeted by a member of the congregation, who explained that they'd just finished a wedding and were preparing for an evening event. My first impression of the building was of light and space; it was radiant in the afternoon light. My friend Andy took my picture, standing in front of the huge icon behind the presider's chair. In the photo, you can see a look on my face that speaks to the experience of beauty: I was flabbergasted, eyes and smile wide. I was in a place that was beautiful in a way I'd never seen, only imagined a church could be. Later, I learned that the building was designed to amplify the experience of beauty.

St. Gregory's building is divided into two areas, one for the Liturgy of the Word of God and the other for the Liturgy of the Table. The arrangement of each room is based on both a functional and a theological expectation of the liturgy. You walk through the great wooden doors of the church building into the area set aside for the altar. It sits alone in the center of the room, an octagonal space filled with sunlight, some sixty feet across and three stories tall. On the base of the altar, facing the entrance, is carved and gilded a verse in Greek from the fifteenth chapter of Luke's gospel: "This guy welcomes sinners and dines with them." On the opposite side of the altar, facing the doors to the outdoor baptismal font, are similarly carved words from the seventh-century bishop and theologian Isaac of

Nineveh: "Did not our Lord share his table with tax collectors and harlots? So then, do not distinguish between worthy and unworthy, all must be equal in your eyes to love and serve." These two inscriptions told me everything that I needed to know about the congregation's dedication to disruption for the sake of the gospel. The beauty that I first encountered continues to dazzle me today. Every time I walk into the church, it is just like that first time: I'm overcome by beauty. As I gaze on the beauty that surrounds me, I am aware of the fact that I am made more beautiful by my presence in that space. All I have to do is look at it, and I am changed.

Beauty approaches us in what is familiar and in what is strange. Welcoming what is beautiful opens us to the presence of God. It's like a dance: God comes to us with promises of love, and we turn to God trusting the truth of that promise. In this dance, a new intelligence is created in us; a new way of knowing the world is born in us. As we are turned into the beauty that we behold, we begin to see the world as a place where the struggle for beauty is worth the trouble. We recognize a responsibility to work for the sake of what is not already beautiful in the world. We are moved to act for the sake of beauty in the world, experiencing transformation along the way.

At St. Gregory's, we use real stuff to adorn the building: textiles from West Africa, vestments made by members, icons painted by hand. We strive to show the universal nature of the Church by using cultural objects from many different places, traditions, and faiths. Instead of following some church supply catalog's idea of appropriate canonical décor, we choose what appeals to our senses. Sometimes this results in an over-the-top aesthetic that challenges a received sense of what churches should use, like the time we choose a Bollywood theme for Christmas. Looking at the yards of bright sari fabric, processional umbrellas from the Church of South India, and mirrored disco ball over the crèche, my colleague Sara Miles beamed, "God loves tacky!" More often, we keep the disco ball safely stored away. Nevertheless, striving for beauty—even when it goes slightly off the rails—is always worth the risk of tacky. God's presence is revealed in a broad range of beauty. This is the value of beauty in the church: it reveals God in ways that are utterly disarming. We enjoy the presence of beauty in both the liturgy and the material culture of our building, and we seek to express beauty in ways that are authentic to our community. I have learned the power of beauty by sharing ministry with the people of St. Gregory's.

Megan is a young attorney, raised in a conservative Evangelical denomination. Megan's youth was spent with a medical missionary team in Central America. Her cradle denomination emphasized a rationalistic approach to God; beauty took the back seat in matters of faith. She says that St. Gregory's role in her transformation has been opening her to receive new experiences: "St. Gregory's has made me more open-minded, more tolerant." Before coming to St. Gregory's, Megan had already experienced the Episcopal Church's historic emphasis on beautiful liturgy, worship that uses all of our senses, but she told me that she didn't fully appreciate the power of beauty in her life until she came to worship with us. "I had studied art. I had bought into the Episcopalian theory of using all your senses and emotions. But St. Gregory's made that more real, and it was around all the time." Beauty is an everyday kind of thing for us; it is expected, and generously shared with everyone who walks through our doors. The ubiquity of beauty transforms us as it reveals God to us. Beauty isn't something reserved for an elite class of parishioners; everyone gets to make beauty, enjoy beauty, share beauty and learn from beauty. And sometimes beauty pushes us in a way that discomforts us. Beauty raises questions about our faith, our values, and our image of God. The approach of beauty is usually not as dangerous as my Maundy Thursday experience—but beauty has the power to disrupt our preconceptions.

Our congregation is dedicated to a fourth-century bishop

who lived in what is now Cappadocia in Turkey. He helped to write the Nicene Creed. He was deposed for a time because he was a terrible business manager. And he was a mystic. He looked deeply into the spiritual life, and saw something that changed him: at the very center of reality is a dazzling, dark beauty. This, Gregory taught, is the destination of all human striving for God. When we look for God, we don't receive a clear picture as much as a luminous darkness. God's shape is a mystery, always approaching us. Beauty is how God chooses to be known. Gregory taught that God is generous in beauty; God doesn't hoard divine beauty. God uses beauty to reveal the truth of our identity. God's beauty stirs within our hearts and minds, transforming us into beauty. It is God's will that we become beautiful, just as God is beautiful. This is our natural state: we are God's creatures, made in God's image, destined for beauty.

In our congregation, we strive to see God in what is beautiful, recognizing that it is in our striving that we will catch the same vision that Gregory saw. We experience beauty doing the same kinds of things that most congregations do: singing in worship, looking at liturgical art, admiring the giftedness of each other, laughing over familiar stories, serving people who are close to death. But we also experience beauty in unique ways: our singing is all unaccompanied, which means that harmony matters to us. We make a lot of the art that we use for worship and to adorn the building. We also look for beauty in the faces of strangers who come through our doors, not just well-loved friends. We recognize that everyone, regardless of age, has a part to play in bringing beauty to birth. We sing to newborns and gather to sing at the deathbeds of our beloved. In all of this, we look for beauty with a sense of delight and wonder. We press into the promise that God longs to take what we offer and use it to reveal just how beautiful the world can be, even when it isn't the most obvious thing in the world.

I have pretty obnoxious habits in museums; I like to start at the end of the exhibition instead of following the recommended route. I love to stare at a single painting for an uncomfortably long time. A few years ago I was at the Louvre in Paris and had that experience of watching people looking at famous works of art through their cell phones. Everyone was crammed together in front of Mona Lisa, trying to get as close as they could, even taking selfies in front of the silently smiling face. I guess you can see a work of art while taking a picture of it through your cell phone, but you'll never really see it. I doubt that a casual, unthinking glance can show us beauty. Beauty is complex, not always pleasant, and frequently challenges us to reconsider our self-understanding. The beauty of God revealed in the world sometimes isn't all that pretty. As a fellow student once told me, "Art doesn't match your sofa." The unreflective admiration of beautiful objects can't take us very deeply into transformation. We have to lose ourselves to see beauty.

On the same trip to Paris, Grant and I met my friend Alice and her family at the Grand Palais to see an installation about light and motion entitled *Dynamo*. There were pieces that you just looked at as well as interactive pieces. One of these interactive pieces was an enclosure, set up in the middle of a bright gallery. You entered the enclosure through a long passageway—covered on all four sides. The further along you went, the dimmer the light became. Then the corridor made a sharp right turn, and then a sharp left turn—like a maze. The light continued to dim until there was no light at all. There were no instructions on this art installation, just a title in French that I couldn't read. The enclosure was full of people—I assume it was full of people, I could hear them even if I couldn't see them. Grant was in front of me, and I kept my hand on his shoulder. I decided that the way to experience this dark space was to stay right next to the wall and follow it around until I came to the corridor that had brought me into the darkness.

But the installation seems to have been designed to make this difficult; there were irregular angles and different lengths of wall. As I walked—somehow—I had the distinct experience of being lost. I couldn't tell where I was, how far from the entrance, it was completely dark. At some point, I took my hand off Grant's shoulder, and when I reached out again, he wasn't there. Now, I'm the kind of person with a remarkably good sense of direction and space. If I look at a map once, I'm usually good finding my destination. But in the dark, twisting enclosure I had no idea where I was. I just surrendered to the darkness. In that darkness, I had no mental map. I had to give up on my self-understanding and ability to control circumstances. Instead of being certain of where I was going or how it was all going to turn out, I simply had to be in the moment, in the dark, trusting that a way would open. It was a very well-designed art installation.

I kept walking in the dark enclosure—trying not to bump into anyone—listening to people speaking French. I was calm, as mindful as I could be. I knew a way would open. After a time that I couldn't gauge, I came at last to a point where the darkness seemed less dim, which led me to more light until I found my way out of the enclosure. There were Grant and Alice and her family, patiently waiting for me. "What took you so long?" Alice asked. "I couldn't find my way," I replied. That was the truth—I couldn't find my way, but the way found me. And although I had felt at ease being present in the darkness, having little control, trusting that a way would open, in the light I could feel my need to stay in control quickly return. In that slightly scary, fully disorienting darkness I was found by beauty. I became the object that beauty wanted to uncover.

God's revelation brings beauty. This is more than a claim about the meaning of beauty, more than an aesthetic hope. The encounter with beauty is not only a gift *from* God; it is an experience *of* God. Beauty is the glory of God, not only a way that we talk about God's glory. Whenever and wherever God is present, there is beauty. Along with this coming of beauty, there is the promise of transformation. God is making a new creation, and it is always beautiful. When we respond to beauty, we find once again that we are destined for beauty.

✂

Artists point us to beauty. My earliest calling was to making beauty. I took my first painting class when I was ten years old. Making beauty was a quiet place for me in the midst of a busy, chaotic, happy family. It wasn't only while painting that I sensed this quiet. I would busy myself during worship at my childhood church by endlessly drawing on the back of the bulletin. I would doodle in the margins of my schoolbooks and come home from class only to spend more time drawing. While my peers would play football in the yard, I would create dollhouses for my sisters. I would invent things that had no purpose but to be beautiful. I kept going because the stillness of making beauty was an access point for God. But it wasn't only making beauty that connected me to God; being in the presence of beauty drew me to the divine. Whether it was found in nature, or art, or music, beauty led me into the mystery of God. I didn't realize it at the time, but beauty taught me to pray. Beauty transformed my life.

Many members of St. Gregory's are artists, working both as amateurs and professionals in a variety of media. There are painters, musicians, singers, actors, writers, poets, tech artists, textile artists, graphic artists, performance artists, and people whose art I am still coming to understand. These artists adorn the building with their work, sometimes unbeknownst to anyone else. It's like the time that Susan stenciled the word SHINE in gold leaf on our outdoor font. At first I thought, "That's cool! Gold leaf on dark green stone—beautiful!" But the work of art continued to teach me, changing my perception of light and water and baptism. The font recirculates water from a catch basin; living water is always flowing from the rock. As the water washed over the gold leaf, it slowly wore away, flowing into the basin from which we baptize. The word was swept into the water. It became a part of the water that washes over those we baptize. We shine with the light of Christ. We are turned into the light that we behold. The meaning of Susan's work kept creeping up on me, surprising me with its subtle genius. Artists help the whole congregation appreciate the power of beauty in the ways that we make community, adorn our building, and plan our ministries.

Betsy is one of the rare St. Gregory's members raised in the Episcopal Church. She is an architect who has a serious avocation as an artist. She came to the congregation after moving to the Bay Area from the East Coast. In her former parish, she made liturgical art for the use of the congregation, but her efforts were not without risk. She told me, "For several years when I first started doing liturgical arts, they got me in trouble. Big trouble." Although she generously offered her work for the church's use, Betsy's art was not always warmly embraced. She told me that some members of her former parish didn't consider her work "Anglican" enough. "Artists often say, 'Art doesn't matter! Nobody cares!' but they haven't done anything for churches. People in churches have intense feelings about what is right and what is wrong for their church."

The response to Betsy's work in her previous congregation was not based on moral conviction, but concerned taste and opinion. Her experience at St. Gregory's has given Betsy a new perspective on herself and her abilities. She describes her experience of transformation as one that involves her work as an artist: "I would never have done all this stuff if it hadn't been for St. Gregory's." When artists share their work with us, they find that the church can be a place that nurtures their creative efforts instead of blocking them. Art is normal for us. It isn't something that only a select group gets to make; everyone can offer their work to reveal the beauty of God in the community. Making art is a normal part of our community's life. There is always an expectation of beauty at St. Gregory's, pointing us to God.

Among the many beautiful things that fill our eyes at St.

Gregory's is our collection of Russian-style icons. We use them both as objects of beauty, and as points of contact between this world and eternity. We respond affectionately to them: people kiss the icons when they enter the building. Members of the church paint most of the icons that we use, under Betsy's leadership. Betsy took her first class in iconography before she came to St. Gregory's. She took a week-long course at Princeton from a Russian iconographer, who himself looked like an ancient saint. "I just fell in love with it and wanted to continue," Betsy explained. She took another course, and another, eventually becoming quite accomplished. After a few years at St. Gregory's, she decided to organize an icon course with the same teacher. People gathered inside the church to paint for nine hours a day, all week long. By the end of the week, the seed for St. Gregory's icon painting group began to grow. Today, a dozen or more men and women gather twice a month in the church to paint. "It's very nice to have permission to create beauty," Betsy explains.

Painting icons is not an easy process; it takes hundreds of hours and skill that's only acquired by the discipline of painting many icons. It is meticulous work that takes a steady hand and a ready heart. Betsy takes the art of painting icons seriously and lovingly; her work adorns the church. Before these icons, beeswax candles glow, catching the gold halos around the saints' heads. Every Sunday, I watch as Betsy slowly walks through the church carrying a lit taper, lighting candles at the icons. "I like to go light the candles; it's a great pleasure to me. And I see icons I have painted and others have painted and that gives me a lot of pleasure."

Her life has not been easy. Recently, Betsy moved into a retirement center, leaving behind the home studio where she spent hours painting the saints. Not long after, she fell and broke both of her wrists. I stopped by the icon group two weeks later. Betsy sat at her usual table, both her wrists in splints. She had set out an icon she'd been working on when she fell.

Although she couldn't manage to hold a brush, she looked at the wood panel, partially covered in egg tempera. Her eye, as trained at seeing as her hands are at painting, rested on the image. I thought about an earlier conversation we'd had about making art and running the risk of offending people with what you make. I asked her, "So is the danger that is implicit in art—is it worth the cost?" She replied, "To me it is."

Beauty is risky. Beauty makes us vulnerable; it opens us to something that we cannot completely hold or control. There is a wild, free quality to beauty that can sometimes shock us. In his poem *Vertue*, George Herbert described the experience of encountering beauty: "Sweet rose, whose hue angrie and brave bids the rash gazer wipe his eye." Beholding beauty changes us: we sigh, we weep, we look away for embarrassment or awkwardness. Beauty is costly; it calls us to see the world in new ways, ways that are tempered by the beauty that we behold. We cannot unsee beauty that has been deeply seen. This is one of the reasons that beauty has the power to transform us. Like staring at a bright light that leaves a shadow on our vision when we look away, beauty remains in our vision long after we behold it.

In many places, art and religion exist in tension. For many, art raises uncomfortable questions about taste, social status, and class. For some congregations, the very idea of "wasting" resources on what is beautiful is offensive. For these people, too much attention to beauty means that there is nothing left with which to address social need. But the everyday occurrence of beauty reveals God in the world. When we pay attention to beauty, we are transformed. Our longing for beauty works within us, revealing who we are and what is beautiful in the world around us.

✖

Beauty draws us to justice. Several times a year, we take the beauty of our liturgy out onto our neighborhood streets.

Sanford Dole, our music director, uses a red cheerleader megaphone to sing out verses to which the congregation responds. We carry processional umbrellas from both the Mar Thoma Church and the Ethiopian Orthodox Tewahedo Church. We beat on drums, African djembes, and Celtic bodhráns, making as much noise as we can, occasionally with a little bit of cowbell. Half a dozen of us are vested in the brightest colors and most exotic textiles we have. Children dance and elders wave palms, or their hands, in the air. We sing and laugh and demonstrate peace. In a city that is completely at home with street protests and pride parades, St. Gregory's processions are designed to use human bodies to experience and manifest God's action in the world.

Our processions are a public performance, witnessed by our neighbors who may have no other experience of the church. People walking by join us in these demonstrations of beauty, taking palm fronds from children and waving them in the air. Outdoor processions, like the Aztec dancers in front of the police station or the Good Friday Stations of the Cross praying at murder sites in the Mission, stake a claim for justice in the neighborhood. We are all there to demonstrate that San Francisco is a place where God's mission is not just inside church walls but is alive in the streets. In our song and dance and joy, we share the invitation of Jesus Christ to join us in remaking the world in peace. We use the beauty that we have to open a new vision of what is happening in the world right now: the gospel is spreading like a burning fire throughout time and space, and everyone is invited to participate. Instead of trying to compel people to take part in these public liturgies, we hold them lightly, even playfully. Liturgy, as an experience of beauty, invites people to recognize their own beauty. John, a painfully shy and completely earnest parishioner, says that our processions "make a lot of difference, and give a lot of visibility" to our life together. Even though John usually chooses to sit quietly in the back, and would die rather than pray out loud in church, on days where we process in the streets, he takes his place in the intense, joyful scrum.

The experience of beauty creates a longing for beauty, and the desire to experience even more beauty. Beauty is expansive. The experience of a beautiful object evokes a desire to tell others about it. This experience begins as we make an aesthetic judgment; we take our own pleasure in beauty seriously as a way to see what is true and real. When we share beauty with other people, it moves us toward a deeper appreciation of truth. In turn, this appreciation moves us toward a passion for justice. When we behold beauty, it creates a heightened attention to harmony, balance, symmetry, and fairness. All of these phenomena are offended by injustice in the world. Like Gregory of Nyssa, the scholar Elaine Scarry links the relationship between beauty and our becoming beautiful. She goes further by describing the intersection of beauty and justice. She claims that beauty assists us in paying attention to justice. First, the beholder of beauty is stirred, by the appearance of beauty, to bring some new beauty into being. Second, the beholder of beauty becomes beautiful as part of his or her inner experience. Finally, beauty and the beholder each affirms the aliveness of the other. When the other person is so affirmed, there is an imperative to work for the sake of justice in the world.

Scarry is not alone in describing the relationship between beauty and justice. John De Gruchy is a South African theologian who has reflected deeply on the power of beauty in transforming human life. His experience is formed by his work in apartheid South Africa. He contrasts the natural beauty of his homeland with the ugliness created by the apartheid regime. This alternate, ugly reality is created by the sins of racism, greed, oppression, and alienation. This ugliness was manifest in the architecture and urban planning that intended to separate South Africans by race. In this environment, intentionally designed to deprive people of beauty, a culture was transformed in the anti-apartheid struggle. De Gruchy writes,

"Whatever else is said about the power of beauty, it has the ability to enhance life, to improve its quality. There is, we might say, a strange necessity for beauty."[1]

There is a disruptive quality to beauty. Beauty must be partnered with truth and justice if it is to have any integrity. Without beauty, truth and justice are each diminished, and the experience of them is attenuated in human life. There is something about beauty that works to free people from the weight of ugliness and attune them to the realities of truth and justice. Beauty feeds that hunger in the human soul created by injustice, despair, indifference, and degradation. Beauty has the power to move the church from the safety of its four walls into the world, working for the sake of the gospel. Beauty has the power to refocus our vision so that we can begin to see the world as God sees it.

It must be recognized that the power of beauty to reveal God is not untouched by human sin. We can view something through the deformed perception of sin and see the truly ugly as beautiful. Thus, we must look to beauty from a God's eye view. God is freely revealed in our experiences, but the shape of the sacred story points to God's revelation within a particular range of human experience: walking in the garden in the cool of the day, rescuing an enslaved people from captivity, dying on a Roman cross. God's beauty is seen most consistently in the merciful, the humble, the poor, the steadfast, and the forsaken. The glory of God is always contained within the context of those the world calls "losers."

Beauty is not an optional tool in our participation in God's mission; it is a vital part of Christian formation. Beauty seeks us out to give an alternative vision of reality from the one that is offered by a culture that seeks to corrupt and destroy God's creation. The church's work is to pay attention to beauty, to use

---

1   John W. de Gruchy, *Christianity, Art and Transformation: Theological Aesthetics in the Struggle for Justice* (Cambridge: Cambridge University Press, 2001), 77.

its power to grow into the royal priesthood of Christ. Beauty invites us to consider the world in new ways, to work as God's people in new ways. When the experience of beauty moves us, we can begin to see the world as God sees it, and then take that vision as a still point from which to work for the sake of God's purpose.

�֍

Hunger drives us toward beauty. The presence of beauty serves those who come with a hunger for transformation. When we recognize our hunger for it, the encounter with beauty can change everything. All that we have to do is receive the gift that God gives. Noreen came to St. Gregory's from the Roman Catholic Church. She entered the convent as a young woman and served many years as a pastoral associate in a parish across the Bay from San Francisco. Although she remembers her former church as a place where she felt cared for and honored, when she came to St. Gregory's, Noreen told me that she was sensory-starved. "In many ways, I had a hard time getting how much I needed good music and good art for my spirit." Although she loved her former parish, Noreen was starving for beauty. Her discontent was a part of the process of her transformation. Any process of transformation begins similarly. If we don't appreciate that we are in some crisis, we have little motivation for change. As Noreen became aware of her dissatisfaction with the role of beauty in her former denomination, she chose to affiliate with a congregation that places a premium on the experience of beauty in the life of the church. Impoverished aesthetics starve the soul; beauty serves people as they make meaning in their lives.

One Sunday, I walked into the church and found a half dozen small icons spread out on a table by the entrance. "We brought those to give away," Joseph told me. The icons were reproductions, lovely copies of ancient masterpieces. One, in particular, the *Virgin of Tenderness*, caught my eye. It is the icon of Mary holding the infant Jesus close to her, their faces pressed together. Jesus's tiny hand is wrapped around Mary's neck. It is an archetypal image of divine embrace. People would approach the table and look at the icons, wondering as I had what they were doing there. "Take one," I'd say. "Someone brought them for you to take home." Noreen found a particular icon, the one that I had first noticed, the *Virgin of Tenderness*. "That's the one that is the most centering of all the icons in the church." I loved the ability to feed Noreen's hunger with the generosity of one of our members. Two weeks later, Noreen told me, "Since I got the icon, it has been very central to my prayer. It felt like a personal gift. Which is the other thing at St. Gregory's: I feel like there's just such an abundance of freedom—the freedom to be here without expectation." Beauty is always full of generosity and freedom; it simply comes to us in our lives, sometimes randomly, sometimes after much searching. In each instance, the approach of beauty comes to fill us with the fullness of God's glory.

✄

Harmony expresses beauty for us. One of the ways that St. Gregory's differs from many other congregations is that all of our singing is unaccompanied. There's no organ in the back of the room or praise band in the front. Instead of relying on accompanying instruments to lead our singing, we just sing, usually in four-part harmony. Making music this way is a very physical experience; you can hear yourself, and the people around you, singing. You can feel the music resonating in your whole body. Since the choir sits amongst the congregation, there is always a strong singer nearby. When we sing in harmony, it is astonishingly beautiful. In the same way that Elaine Scarry describes the experience of beauty as an influence on the perception of justice, we have found the experience of singing in harmony transformational as a community. It has become a metaphor for our whole life together. The harmony of the music, and the relationships of those who make the music, is an enacted parable of the Kingdom of God. We listen to each other carefully. We pay attention to the tempo, because if we don't the music begins to drag painfully.

Harmony in the congregation's singing is an experience of beauty, as well as an organizing principle. For many, it has become a metaphor for their ministries. Like many congregations, St. Gregory's falls into the trap of having one person do the same job repeatedly over the years. Elizabeth has organized our annual Palm Sunday breakfast for years. She has been a member of St. Gregory's for more than twenty years. She is the kind of church member who does everything, a realist with a huge heart and a keen eye. She also has a sense that for the harmonious operation of the community to continue, she has to give her work away. The last time that she led the breakfast team, she recruited Joanna to be her assistant, as well as to take her job the next year. Taking the long view, Elizabeth understands that sharing responsibility is one way to work for harmony in the congregation. The way that she describes her experience of the building on a Sunday morning is the same as her sense of how to organize the ministries we share. "I try to look at our church as a stranger would see it. Does that look right? Does it look balanced? Is there something uneven? Is it jarring?" Not only do we work to create a sense of beauty and harmony in our physical space, but we also seek to create harmony in sharing the work of ministry. Creating an atmosphere that is hospitable and welcoming to new members, sharing work with them, and knowing when it's time to let go of a ministry—all are expressions of harmony in our life as a congregation.

I received her phone call while I was picking up some bookcases for the church. At first, all I could make out was sobbing. Jessica, a former banker who loves to sing in our choir, had just been diagnosed with macular degeneration. "How am I going to be able to read the music? How will I do anything that I love?"

I talked to her on my cell phone as I drove back across the Bay Bridge to San Francisco. "You're going to be okay. We're going to make it through this together." Being a person who treasures my sense of sight, I was deeply empathetic to her plight; being someone whose family has a history of the same disease, I was frightened. "Let's pray right now," I said to Jessica. I prayed for her, for peace and stillness and healing. By the time the call was over, her husband had made it to her side.

A woman of vast energy and wide-ranging interests, Jessica has lost almost half her sight in the past five years. What was initially a crisis for her has become an opportunity to be formed in new ways; she has gained a new vision as she has lost her sight. She has developed a deep, spiritual, almost mystical appreciation of beauty and harmony. The intersection of art, music, liturgy, and relationships creates something that is greater than the sum of the parts for Jessica. Any single aspect of beauty may be, in itself, aesthetically pleasing, but the interaction of each piece provides opportunities for transformation. Jessica says of her experience of transformation at St. Gregory's, "What I've learned is not to judge myself, to be more gentle with myself in creating beauty." For Jessica, harmony is the essence of our life in the liturgy. "It's very beautiful. It's like a multi-sensory Eucharist. The whole thing becomes the bread and wine. It gets bigger. It's the majesty of all of the things we can do to glorify Spirit and God." Harmony connects everything. The experience of beauty is more than a collection of different beautiful objects and events. Beauty is in the way that each piece relates to every other part.

※

Human beings are beautiful. Although we may seek to dodge the fact, or cover over the fact with a false self-image, we human beings are fundamentally beautiful, and our relationships reveal beauty. The whole history of our salvation rests on the claim that our value cannot be questioned. After their fall from grace, when God seeks after the first man and woman, it is not to destroy them but to clothe them. Our long walk back to Eden is on a pathway smoothed by God's love and mercy. We never walk this pathway alone: the beauty of being human is perfected in communion with others. The relationships that we enjoy are not optional for us; they make us who we are. We are beautiful, reflecting the beauty that comes from God. The co-founder of St. Gregory's, Richard Fabian, writes that our motivation for staying in relationship with each other is seeing God at work in the other's life: "We follow Jesus's example, not only because he was good and noble, but because we believe the love he showed us is the foundation plan of the world and the true principle of our being. Through sin we lost sight of this principle, and wrestled darkly with our pain and fear, destroying one another and wrecking our world. But God revealed his loving plan to us anew, in a way even our blindness could see."[2]

God's loving plan includes the potential for each one to see the other not as a rival, but as one who is beautiful and can be known. Again and again, people at St. Gregory's have told me that they experience personal relationships with other members as locations of beauty. Sharing in relationship offers us a new way of understanding beauty. When we recognize beauty in the people that we encounter at church, week after week we learn to see more and more of the image of God. One way that I see this is in the way that children and adults are together in the liturgy. The whole community gathers for liturgy on Sunday; there is not a separate space for children or youth during the service. Our expectation is that children and youth will join, both as leaders and participants, in the liturgy. For some, this can be a challenge.

Sometimes kids want to be somewhere other than worship. On those Sundays when I'm not assigned to preach or preside

---

2   Richard Fabian, *Plan for the Mission of St. Gregory of Nyssa*, unpublished manuscript, San Francisco, December 1977.

in the liturgy, I observe what's going on around the church. Sometimes I'll see a kid sitting alone in the rotunda while the rest of the congregation is in the seating area. One Sunday in Lent, I sat down on the edge of a platform next to Max, a smart, creative preteen. "What are you reading?" I asked. He looked at me, bored, and showed me the cover of his book. "I'm glad that you're here," I said. He rolled his eyes but didn't walk away. It takes patience and love to welcome preteens into the liturgy on their terms, seeing them as they really are, not as the rector might want them to be. Max just isn't interested in worship, but he comes and stays in the room with the rest of the congregation, quietly reading. The beautiful thing is his presence, not his living into my expectations.

Over the years, Megan has worked with young people in the congregation. She will sometimes sit with a group of young people during the liturgy, not to supervise them, but because she values their companionship. Megan tells me that this is an opportunity for her to deepen her relationship with young people. "Having young people come to rely on me is a beautiful thing. You know, having students who are having a hard time in service sit near you or ask you to put your hand on their back and quiet them down, is helpful and satisfying." Megan's ministry with the young people of St. Gregory's is more than a job that the community needs someone to do; it is beautiful.

⌘

Beauty challenges us to appreciate difficulty. Difficult beauty, as defined by Bernard Bosanquet, includes events, people, and objects that are both beautiful and difficult to appreciate in conventional terms of beauty. Sometimes, the encounter with difficult beauty is utterly surprising.

There is a spice store near my house, a kind of boutique for people who like to cook. Since I like to cook, I go in a couple of times a year and restock my spice rack. The store is a minimalist design: white walls and black floors with cubbies of glass spice jars around the edge. Each cubby has a jar of spice that you can sample before you make a purchase. The spice store has the expected things, oregano, and vanilla, but they also have unexpected things—things that you didn't know you needed like umami powder and piment d'Espelette. The other day, I was walking by the spice store. I went in and smelled the contents of the jars, pungent and sweet, hot and grassy. Some of the smells evoke familiar memories, others bring back more ancient memories. It was all beautiful in an utterly conventional way: lovely smells in a pleasant space.

Walking back to my house, I saw a man walking toward me. I didn't think much of it until he came close to me on the sidewalk. I noticed a teardrop tattoo beneath his left eye. And then I caught his smell: an unwashed body, familiar and ancient—not unpleasant, but unexpected—difficult. He smelled like cumin and smoke, the way my grandfather smelled when he stopped washing. That smell brought a memory of the love that bound me to my grandfather, even when his personality was deconstructed by dementia. At that moment, I thought that this smell of an unwashed body was just as beautiful as the most exotic scent of cinnamon and grains of paradise. Spices and bodies. Sweet and savory. A stranger on the street and the memory of my grandfather. All of these were surprisingly mixed up in me. I didn't expect to encounter beauty that afternoon, walking the neighborhood on my day off. I didn't imagine that a stranger's unwashed body might be a source of beauty. I didn't consciously go seeking beauty; rather, beauty sought me. The encounter with beauty changed my perception and forced me to question what was truly beautiful in the world. This is the way that beauty works on the human soul. Just when you least expect it, beauty approaches, challenging what you had thought was long settled in yourself. Beauty can unmake prejudgments and expand your vision of the world that God loves. Maybe this is why the church, although dependent on beauty, sometimes lives in tension with it: the presence of beauty in our lives may mean that we have to tear up our plans and start being the church in a new kind of way.

One of my favorite parishioners—one who epitomized difficult beauty—was Lynn. Born with a congenital disease, *osteogenesis imperfecta*, or brittle bone disease, she died in 2014. Lynn spoke in a Tennessee drawl liberally peppered with southernisms—particularly when she wanted to shock her audience. "Darlin' I was *born* with broken arms," she explained to me soon after we met. I was seldom shocked by her. Being raised in Gulf Coast Texas, I understand the ways that Southern women of a certain generation make up for the denial of their own power. Lynn tried to shock me because it had become a habit, a way of not disappearing in the crowd. Lynn's condition resulted in tiny, twisted arms and legs. Her nails were usually painted bright yellow. She was confined to a motorized wheelchair that once gave out during our Palm Sunday procession around the block. "Just push me up the damn hill," she told the ushers. Because she lived so much of her life on the border between what people consider "normal" and "disabled," she was keenly aware of strangers and offering them a welcome at St. Gregory's. Lynn was also a photographer, taking as her vantage point the wheelchair in which she spent most of her time.

Randy came to St. Gregory's after Hurricane Katrina destroyed his home in New Orleans. An elegant man with a waxed mustache, Randy told me that, in his estimation, the most beautiful aspect of St. Gregory's was Lynn. "The joy that this twisted body contained was unbelievable. And that through her lens she was showing me all these different aspects of beauty. I have two of her photographs framed and hanging on my wall. Beauty through her eye. The welcoming world through her eye. And there was such an important place for her in our church." Randy reflects that beauty is found in "all the different places where light shines." In addition to the icons and artwork, and our beautiful building, the light also shines through the people who constitute the community of St. Gregory's, including the people who are not conventionally beautiful. People who would normally have little reason to interact form relationships as a result of making church together. These relationships nurture our transformation as we live together in our mutual oddness.

The church is one of the only places in our society where we are together with people who are different from us. The church welcomes differences of experience, age, sexual orientation, economic class, and theological understanding. All of these differences reveal the beauty of God that we each reflect. Our differences also drive us to distraction. Adults who are unused to children sometimes find young people annoying; young people find that some adults are demanding and rigid. People on the Left don't understand people on the Right. New members question the norms established by tenured members, and on and on and on. Our differences cannot be ignored; they matter to the whole church, even when they annoy us. Finding beauty in relationship to others is not always a simple process; it challenges our sense of autonomy and personal choice. Mark, a bookish gay man who can quote lines from any classic movie, says that this tension is itself beautiful. "For me, the most beautiful things are not perfect and pristine; they're marred, they show rough edges, sweat, and pain. One of the things I like a lot at St. Gregory's is when there's roughness."

The beauty of persons and relationships is not idealized; it is real, messy, and relational. People can be difficult to relate to, and for some congregation members, this difficulty outweighs the benefit of being in a relationship. For some, sharing relationships only makes sense with those who are familiar. Such a limited experience of relationships is normal for many, but those relationships don't have the same kind of power as relationships with those who are unlike us. Real, deep beauty is found in welcoming what is difficult. As different people are knit together in relationship, beauty is created, God is revealed, and transformation is empowered.

✳

Regardless of its approach, beauty works for our transformation. The people of St. Gregory's have taught me that beauty is a fundamental part of the spiritual life. Although working in the church to make beauty is sometimes a risk, the power of beauty is worth the challenge. When we gratefully accept the gifts of beauty brought into the church and encourage our members to actively engage beauty in their lives, transformation happens. Beauty inspires and feeds the human soul, which is why people come to church: they are starving spiritually. Whether it is singing in harmony, forging new relationships, or painting icons, taking an active role in making beauty transforms congregations. All of these experiences show the beauty of God, alive and present in the community.

One of the hymns we sing is a paraphrase of Gregory of Nyssa's writings: "God creates life; life beholds beauty; beauty begets love; love is the life of God." The original words of Gregory are, "For the life of the Supreme Being is love, seeing that the Beautiful is necessarily lovable to those who recognize it, and the Deity does recognize it, and so this recognition becomes love, that which He recognizes being essentially beautiful."[3] Gregory's teaching concerns the resurrection of the body and the meaning of desire, love, faith, and beauty in eternal life. He taught that, above all human experiences, there is love that lasts into eternity because it is the essence and nature of God. When all else passes away, love remains the eternally vivacious aspect of what it means to be human. According to Gregory, with love, there is also beauty. There is beauty because whatever God recognizes is essentially beautiful. Beauty draws forth love from the beholder in a dynamic that is the substance of eternal life. In this mortal life, there is beauty and love, imperfectly shared

---

3 Gregory of Nyssa, "On the Soul and the Resurrection," New Advent, Church Fathers, http://www.newadvent.org/fathers/2915.htm (accessed March 3, 2014).

among human beings. Nevertheless, it is the same beauty and love that are completed in God's eternal life, shared freely with all humankind. The presence of beauty, along with love, is a guarantee of eternal life. Beauty and love have eternal meaning. The hope of transformation promised in the resurrection is what Christians hope for in the last day. Until then, beauty serves as a pledge of that hope.

chapter

2

Social Engagement: Overcoming Alienation with Love

God is at work here, and I feel
that it's going to make a difference
all the way around and in other ways
—in a lot of people's lives.

—Elizabeth B.

SOMETIMES BEING YOKED to Jesus, and walking the pathway that he chooses, takes you to some pretty weird places. A couple of years ago, I was in North Carolina at the Wild Goose Festival—what somebody described as a "Christian Woodstock." It's a justice, spirituality, and art festival that's been around for a few years. I've been to four of them. In 2014, I presided at the closing Eucharist for the Festival. Right before the closing the final speaker, Rev. William Barber—the man who started the Moral Mondays movement in North Carolina, a tall, solemn African American; a fervent preacher and prophet—had an altar call. About 250 people came forward for prayer, including me. I wrapped my arm around a man with whom I had a passing acquaintance and a lingering disagreement, bowed my head, and prayed to be healed.

We didn't go straight to the altar after the altar call. We started with a gospel music sing-a-long lead by Rev. Yolanda, a six-foot-tall, gospel-singing drag queen in a gold lamé animal print gown. Then I belted out the prayer that we chanted at the beginning of every Sunday liturgy at St. Gregory's, "Blessed be God the Word, who came to his own and his own received him not—for in this way God glorifies the stranger. O God, show us your image in all who come to us today, that we may welcome them and you." Then after Scripture reading and more singing, Sara Miles took the stage to preach. After the sermon, we moved to the altar table, set in the middle of the field in front of the stage, covered in baskets of bread and mason jars of wine. I chanted the Eucharistic prayer, and people took the bread and wine and shared them freely with the neo-hippie carnival performers and the black grandmothers, the post-evangelicals and the southern Evangelicals, the queers and the frat boys, the babies and the elders. You know—it was like church. And it was the heavenly Jerusalem, come down from heaven once again into our midst. Rev. Barber was there, taking the bread from Sara, and a neo-hippie wearing deer antlers on his dreadlocked head was there taking a mason jar of wine from me. It was beautiful.

Until it was over. As I walked away from the eucharistic field, I heard a prominent leader in American Christian culture say to someone in the crowd, "You know, I'm all for marriage equality, but the gay issue is escalating the religious war in this country." Like he hadn't witnessed what we had just made together: straight Christians and queer Christians together at Christ's table. His opinion was disconnected from the beauty that had accompanied us in the liturgy. His fear dominated his joy. While everybody else was mashed in love around the altar, his distance from the center point of God's joyful remaking of us startled me. The words of the gospel rang in my ears, "We played the pipes for you, and you wouldn't dance; we sang dirges, and you wouldn't be mourners."[4]

Yet, I believed then, as I do now, that God's promise is sure: wisdom is justified by her deeds. When we engage the world around us, we are transformed by the engagement. When we press through our fear to see the world as God sees it, we are transformed. When we dare to break the rules, to risk respectability, for the sake of God's Commonwealth of Peace, we are transformed.

There is that thing in our carefully constructed culture—even within our congregations—that doesn't like coloring outside the lines. Too often, we like to keep things nice and tidy. And there is something in us that objects to the yoke of Jesus when it takes us to places that we haven't been before—like a Eucharist in a field in North Carolina with a mash-up of unlikely strangers, or a street protest, or a food pantry, or a foot care clinic for homeless men. We may object that the desire of God is too easy, the love of God is too free, and the mercy of God is too simple. The domination culture around us understands that getting things done has nothing to do with the character of God

4   Matthew 11:17, NJB.

and everything to do with the simple application of force, violence, blame, and scapegoating. Sometimes it seems we believe the liberty of God must be stopped at all costs, because if God's offer of freedom is revealed to people, they will see that there is nothing to fear, that the yoke of Jesus will make all of us free.

Jesus offers an alternate reading of history—of my history, of yours—that promises us freedom from what we fear. Jesus says that everyone who is burdened and beaten down by the experiment of living may lay down that burden, lay down the lies with which they have made a life, lay down the fear that God's love is just too embracing, and take up the yoke which leads to the fullness of life, real freedom, and service to all people. God gives us freedom, which our Book of Common Prayer defines so beautifully in the prayer: "O God, who art the author of peace and lover of concord, in knowledge of whom standeth our eternal life, whose service is perfect freedom: Defend us, thy humble servants, in all assaults of our enemies; that we, surely trusting in thy defense, may not fear the power of any adversaries."[5] Jesus gives us a new story in which our peace is secured in service, and peace makes us free. It is in this freedom that we have the power to take up social engagement: our service in the world for Christ's sake.

This is how social engagement becomes an engine of transformation in congregational life: first comes our own desire to see justice in real ways in everyday life. Desire burns in us to the degree that we begin to notice ways that we might serve the cause of God's justice in the world. But that desire itself is not enough. We have to do real work in our lives, doing real service in the same Spirit that drove Jesus to pour out his life for the world. So, we go into the world as servants of God's mission. We experience the lives and needs of other people, perhaps

5 The Episcopal Church, "A Collect for Peace," *The Book of Common Prayer and Administration of the Sacraments and Other Rites and Ceremonies of the Church: Together with the Psalter or Psalms of David According to the Use of The Episcopal Church* (New York: Church Hymnal Corp., 1979), 54.

strangers to us. When we have these experiences, we share them with other people. We may share our experiences with friends and family. Then we find ways to share our experiences with others in our congregation, telling our stories as a part of God's story with us. When we share what we experience in our service to the world, it is an invitation to others to join us in the work. As a result, we begin to see people's lives, their actions, and attitudes, changing. New behaviors, new attitudes grow in us, informing our desire more and more. We continue to share our experiences and reflect on them with other people. Above all, we approach social engagement with humility, trusting that God is already at work making the world anew. This work is not confined to an elite cadre of the congregation; it is something that every member can engage. It is rooted and grounded in love.

⚜

In June 2015, I joined fifteen hundred other Episcopalians marching in the streets of Salt Lake City, protesting our society's addiction to gun violence. It was early enough on a Sunday morning that the heat of the high desert didn't melt us. Along with the other members of the Diocese of California's General Convention deputation, I walked a half-mile from the convention center where we were meeting to a park in the middle of downtown. As we walked, following a mass of crimson-clad bishops, we chanted, *"Out of the deep I call unto thee, O Lord, consider well the sound of my longing soul."* I walked next to my friend AnnaMarie, a gifted singer and fellow deputy. She and I have been friends since I first came to St. Gregory's, where she is a parishioner. AnnaMarie is a former Baptist, a foodie who pickles her own carrots and mixes her own cocktails. We had never protested in the streets together. The only times that we had walked and chanted on city pavement was for St. Gregory's liturgical processions. We walked and chanted, each of us improvising harmony to the simple chant tone we'd been taught. Being taller than most in the procession, I kept an eye on the horizon ahead of us and along the sides of the street where we walked. I wondered what the few people who stood along the route watching thought we were doing.

We arrived at our destination, and I quickly found a shady place to listen to the speakers. They talked about the social cost of gun violence, about the ways that it dehumanizes and objectifies us. Gayle Fisher-Stewart, then a deacon from the Diocese of Washington, had served as an officer with the Metropolitan Police Department in Washington, D.C. She talked about the gun training she had received at the police academy. "We were taught to shoot to kill. Two to the center of mass and if the person did not go down, the next shot went to the head. This is about killing." I imagined the contrasting places in her personal history: a trained killer who had been called to feed God's people the Bread of Heaven. Her courage inspired me, but her history filled me with grief. *Out of the deep I call.*

Although I am opposed to the easy access our society gives to gun ownership, I have fired guns in my life. My brother is an avid gun collector. My nephew is an accomplished hunter. I know the powerful thrill of shooting guns. I am not pure. But I chose to march with my sisters and brothers in the hot streets of Salt Lake City to reaffirm my commitment to peace, to be changed by my actions. Once you stand publicly with others and declare yourself as a certain kind of person, a person of peace, it is hard to retreat into violence again. Using my body as an instrument of protest strengthened my resolve and clarified my self-understanding. It was the entire event that worked this transformation in me: the early morning heat, the mass of Christians walking in the streets, singing the same words over and over, my friendship with AnnaMarie and our shared life in prayer at St. Gregory's, my striving, sweating body, my history, and my resolve.

Social engagement transforms us. It means working with people, both friends and strangers, to construct something new.

Social engagement builds more resilient, sustainable congregations; and it works to free us from fear. While it addresses specific needs, like violence or homelessness or refugee resettlement, social engagement also nurtures relationships among groups and individuals who are strangers to each other. That is to say, it builds the Body of Christ. It takes people who have no reason to know one another and gives them the work of remaking what is broken in the world. This is why social engagement is an engine of transformation.

Before we can work for justice, we have to see people as beautiful, not merely deserving. Our deep longing for justice in the world is met as we make real relationships with others. When we retreat into social isolation, there is an increased suspicion of those who are different. Suspicion leads to prejudice. Prejudice leads to violence. Violence leads to death. Social engagement is a starting point for dismantling violence and insisting that life is more powerful than death. It is about witnessing God's action in the world and then witnessing to it. More than anything, it is about seeing uniqueness, individuality, and unfamiliarity in others as beautiful. Social engagement is empowered by our mutuality, by supporting each other and recognizing our interdependence. This is a powerfully counter-cultural position for most of us.

Social engagement is the first step that the church must take in dismantling violence—both large-scale violence and micro-aggression. Congregations express their own style of social engagement uniquely: some take up direct charitable acts, some work in political activism. Regardless of the particular work that we take up, from feeding the hungry to lobbying elected officials, the best social engagement is both working for change and being changed by the work.

✄

St. Gregory's does not have an outreach committee. There is no official body in the congregation that suggests to our members what they should do to fulfill the gospel's call to serve. Instead, the strength of our social engagement is our shared responsibility for taking on the work. Each of us is responsible for looking at the world around us, finding the places where we want to make a commitment to use our gifts and passions to serve. We find our theological rationale for social engagement in the example of Jesus Christ, who spent his time forgiving sinners, healing the sick, welcoming outcasts, and laying down his life for his friends. The Spirit of Jesus moves us to love and to serve in the same way. So, instead of setting up complicated organizational systems to do Jesus's work, members of the congregation are empowered to fulfill their own need to serve others as we live our lives. The work of ministry is not the responsibility of church professionals, the rector, or any other designated expert; we are all amateurs in the work of ministry. Everyone is competent to love and serve.

We also have a responsibility to share what we are doing with the rest of the congregation, inviting others into the work to which we're committed. Sometimes this means one or two people joining a protest march over institutional violence. Sometimes it means writing letters to city hall about the lack of affordable housing. Sometimes it means starting programs with a long view of social change or joining programs that are already in existence. Sometimes it is doing what we do at our paid jobs: teaching, healing, caring for others. Regardless of the form it takes, our work is an expression of our desire to grow in the Spirit of Jesus and his service to the world. We share our commitments to social change as a part of the Sunday liturgy.

There are two particular moments in the liturgy that, since St. Gregory's founding, have been opportunities for members of the congregation to share their own experiences with social engagement. The first opportunity is called *sermon sharing*. This is a time following the homily when the preacher invites the congregation's response using these words: "We continue the sermon together, sharing our own experiences. So, if you have heard something of your own story in the words this morning, I invite you to stand and share it with the assembly. Listen to each other and listen in the silence, because God is speaking in both." Then the preacher calls on people who are ready to stand and speak. The other opportunity to talk about our work is during the prayers of the people. There is no liturgical leader who reads all of the prayers; we don't use one of the forms in the prayer book. The intercessions are spontaneous, personal expressions of their need and desire. People call out their intercessions, loudly, so they can be heard by everyone in the congregation. Our response to each intercession is, "Lord, have mercy."

Maitreya, an attorney and passionate realist, works for the exoneration of innocent prisoners across the country. She will frequently offer intercession for them during the prayers of the people or talk about her experience of working for their freedom during sermon sharing. She names those whose cases she has tried, rejoicing when they are released from prison and weeping when they are denied their freedom. Unlike most parishioners, her professional life is all about social engagement, about the dismantling of systemic violence. Although she could make more money in other sectors of the legal profession, she has a calling to the work of exonerating the innocent. Whenever Maitreya shares her experience in the liturgy, it deeply touches the members of the congregation. Jessica shared her experience with me: "I think of Maitreya. There are people out there that are doing hard things that are not going to be done by anyone else, looking for justice for the innocents."

It is because of Maitreya's passionate concern for justice, rooted in her daily life, that the people of St. Gregory's are formed in the direction of justice. She brings the concerns of the world into the liturgy in a way that stirs our imaginations to pray and work for justice. The power of her sharing is grounded in her experience; her voice is full of authority and complete authenticity. When she speaks about justice, it is more than an opinion at second hand, more than a factoid from the *New York*

Times or NPR. Lived experience, freely shared face-to-face with people, has the power to transform our experience. People like Maitreya take their engagement in the world and use it as a point of prayer and testimony. God is speaking through their lives and experiences, speaking to the congregation and motivating us to find our work in the world.

When people give testimony to their work in God's mission in the world, it transforms the way that others in the congregation can imagine their social engagement. None of us can do this work alone; no one has the power to sustain themselves alone in working for social change. There will never be a perfect way of responding to God's call to serve the world's need. But when we testify to what we experience in the ambiguity of life, in trust and doubt, in personal relationships and loneliness, in the known and loved, and in strangers, the congregation gains a clearer picture of God's Commonwealth of peace. When we speak our personal experience to others, we tune the whole congregation to social engagement. Noreen affirms her need to hear the testimony of others' experience: "Our prayer really does make a difference. Our connecting in real ways with each other makes a difference in the world." Sharing our experience transforms us.

⚜

Social engagement must be relational. Every Friday, volunteers gather at St. Gregory's to give away groceries, right around the altar in the middle of the church, to four hundred or so hungry people who live in San Francisco. Although it sounds like an easy enough task—give food to hungry people—the actual work of The Food Pantry is back breaking and time consuming. It is also completely invigorating. I am the president of The Food Pantry board, as well as an occasional cook for its volunteers and pastor to all who come. In May 2004, my second Friday at the pantry, I fixed a big pot of beans for lunch. "People can't do this kind of work eating day-old cookies," I explained to Sara, the pantry's founder. "Let's just give them a little something for lunch." The beans were like the ones my mother would cook every Monday when I was growing up, savory and filling.

After lunch, people began coming in to get the free food we give away. About an hour into the service, Sara came up to me and said, "Miss Grace needs you to pray for her." Although she can be pushy, Sara always hits the mark when it comes to someone's need for pastoral attention. I found Miss Grace sitting alone, an overflowing bag of produce by her side. A woman in her seventies, a devout Pentecostal, she has lived with tragedy as a constant companion in her life. "I'm feeling kind of low just now," she explained. "It's about this time of year that I lost my daughter in Jonestown." I could not imagine the pain of losing a child in the jungle of Guyana, cast into the engine of religious violence. I took her hand and began to pray for her. Her hand, small and soft and dark, gripped mine tightly. As I prayed with her, the Spirit came down and prompted Miss Grace to pray in tongues. I'm not a stranger to tongue-speaking, but I didn't expect it to happen that Friday afternoon. I just held on to her hands and waited for her prayer to end and said, "Amen."

Scrubbing the bean pot later that day, I wondered at the blessing of being in such a richly generous place. How is it that I get to spend my time with a stranger, holding her pain in my prayer, being uplifted by our mutual dependence on the God of Jesus Christ? The pantry's choice to give food and prayer away to everyone who comes through the doors has shown me new ways of understanding social engagement. Instead of having to fix the systemic problems of food security, I have to be present in relationship to Miss Grace and feed a hungry crew of workers a pot of beans. The Church does not have to solve every problem that comes to our doorsteps; we just have to look at the world with the compassion of God and then do *something*. We must strive to build relationships among people in the context of a nurturing community.

The Food Pantry at St. Gregory's is such a community. The pantry is a part of a national distribution chain of surplus food. In cities all over the country, large food banks collect surplus food and sell it for pennies on the dollar to non-profit organizations and pantries that feed hungry people. Most of the food distribution centers give food only to those who live in a certain zip code, or who are a certain age, or who meet certain other criteria. The Food Pantry is distinct in San Francisco; early in its history, it chose to give groceries to everyone who comes, regardless of where they live or who they are. No one has to prove worthiness to receive groceries; everyone is welcome to come and get food. This practice is intentionally based on St. Gregory's practice of giving communion to everyone without exception.

Every week hundreds of people are fed. Fresh produce, beans, rice, cereal, and more are set out around the altar and those who come in walk around the table selecting groceries. Many of those who first came to get groceries now run the pantry. Every Friday, I get to witness the power of transformation in the lives of the pantry volunteers: it's all about their hunger. Just as their hunger drew them to the pantry to get food, so their hunger for an experience of community urges them forward. The volunteers feed each other around the altar. They care for each other in sickness. They call people who are absent on a Friday. They welcome others to come and share in the work of giving the food away. They do all of this work, and in doing it, they incarnate the Spirit of Jesus. The pantry accomplishes this goal as it strives to follow the teaching carved on our altar: "Do not distinguish between worthy and unworthy." It is the mutuality of relationship between the volunteers, and those being served, that is the important piece in the process of transformation. Although the work of the pantry is carried out in an orderly fashion, efficiency is not its principal goal. The goal is transformation.

Transformation happens in the lives of people who do not directly participate in the pantry. Most members of St. Gregory's work at least one job; few can take off work to volunteer at the pantry on a Friday. This doesn't stop almost every member of the congregation from taking great pride in the work of the pantry. Just knowing that the pantry is feeding people impresses non-participants. It's like the inspiration you get from some beautiful location you've never seen in person. People read about the pantry, or see videos of it in operation, and are changed by the experience. Noreen, who works as a spiritual director with ongoing Friday commitments, told me that, "Even though I can't participate in The Food Pantry community in a direct way, I feel the importance of that connection: just appreciating that we bring the church to the community and invite the community in a broad way." It's not only in direct participation that the process of transformation takes place; it can begin by appreciating and reflecting on the experience of others engaged in acts of service.

The loving quality of the relationships shared among those who come to volunteer at The Food Pantry could not happen apart from the way we worship. Even though most of the pantry volunteers never join us for worship, the prayer that begins at the altar extends into every part of the congregation's life. We strive to nurture people's spiritual growth in service to others rather than from the sense of entitlement or superiority. Our congregation is formed on the proposition that giving people opportunities to serve others is the surest way to come to spiritual insight and maturity. The pantry both enlivens and changes the experience of worship and the members as worshippers. This claim rests on a core value of St. Gregory's: service to the community and the liturgy of the congregation are a single reality. Social engagement must be more like worship; when it is, transformation happens in people's lives.

✄

Before I came to St. Gregory's, I was the rector of St. Andrew's Church in Houston, Texas. A congregation of dedicated men and women, St. Andrew's has always been a place on the forefront of social engagement. Half a century ago, they worked with other local congregations to build senior housing for vulnerable communities in Houston. Some of their social engagement is closer to the ground; for years they have kept a supply of sack lunches on hand to give to hungry people who come to the church. When I was the rector of St. Andrew's, we were involved in community organizing and pre-school care. I brought many things to St. Andrew's, including my love of icons.

There was a small chapel at St. Andrew's, right off the back entrance of the building. Before it was dedicated as a chapel, it had been a Sunday school classroom, with a low ceiling and an exposed brick wall. Across from the entrance door was a backlit, stained glass image of the Good Shepherd. Trying to make it look less like a repurposed room, I installed several icons on the exposed brick wall. One was a large reproduction of the icon of Jesus, as Pantocrator. He has a rather stern look on his face and cradles a book in his left hand. As with most icons, his gaze is not directly at the viewer, but just beyond—looking at something that is just beyond and ahead of us. I reminded my parishioners, "*Pantocrator* means the guy who holds everything in his hands."

There was a woman who would come to the chapel several times a day. She was homeless for the most part and suffered some mental illness that seemed like schizophrenia. She talked to herself all of the time and layered bright clothing, wrapping her hair in sweaters and shawls like a turban. She was unwashed, but wore bold lipstick and eye shadow; her scent would linger after she left the building. We would try and work with her, but it was hard. She didn't like being pinned down or sharing too much of her life with us. When I asked her name, she would give me one of several. I decided to call her by the name she first used, Sheila. We would give her sack lunches when she came in. I would talk to her a little. Once I got as far as finding her a place to live in a single-room occupancy facility downtown, but she only stayed a day.

I don't know what I thought would happen to Sheila in the long term. I knew she wasn't going to become some kind of housewife driving a Suburban around Houston. I couldn't even tell her age; she might have been twenty-five or forty-five. Like so many living in our obscenely rich culture, she was a poor woman whom the world could just categorize as a street person.

One evening I was at St. Andrew's for a vestry meeting. We sat around an oak table in a large public room down the hall from the chapel. Although we usually kept the door to the parking lot locked, because of our pre-school program, that night it was unlocked, and the chapel door was wide open. Halfway through the meeting, I thought I heard the entrance door open but didn't think much of it. Church business occupied me that night. When I went to the chapel after the vestry meeting, I could tell that Sheila had been there. Her scent hung heavily in the air. I looked behind the pews in the chapel, just to make sure she wasn't sleeping in one of them. Then I noticed something on the icon of Jesus the Pantocrator. At first, I couldn't tell if it was the light reflecting off the paper surface, so I walked up to the icon to get a closer look. Just above Jesus's mouth was a smear of purple lipstick. There is an ancient tradition of kissing icons, but when they're printed reproductions on paper, it can damage the image. I wiped the lipstick stain off and headed home. But the next morning I noticed that there was a definite stain—a kiss that just wouldn't go away. Last summer, when I visited my former parish, I walked into the chapel and saw that the stain on the icon was still there. And driving through Houston that day, more than ten years after I left, I could swear that I saw Sheila, walking along the street, softly speaking to herself.

Social engagement must be relational if it is going to work for our transformation. The work that congregations do is of a different quality than the work of a social service agency. Those agencies are essential to helping people, and can effect change in ways that are profound and necessary. But congregations have a different concern. Our work of social engagement is personal; it is based on our desire to share ourselves with another person and be changed in the process. Social engagement in congregational life must avoid what Peter Buffett describes as "philanthropic colonialism,"[6] an attempt to solve other people's problems with little particular knowledge of or experience in those persons' particular context. Instead, we must strive to understand the ways in which we can, on the basis of our lived experience, enter the world in the Spirit of Jesus who longs to serve all people. Noreen says, "I think that the core of this is not how to figure out how to be more helpful in the world. It's more how to be in the world in a way that is more receptive to being a part of it all."

When congregations take up the work of social engagement, it must begin by attending to the wisdom of those we are called to serve. We must honor the intelligence they have about their own needs, and how to meet those needs. Social engagement with people outside the congregation must reflect the way we want to experience all of our relationships within the congregation: with mutuality, respect, empathy, and love. Janet, a food entrepreneur and choir member, notes that when we take up social engagement, "it's not our place to judge whether people deserve our help." Mercy, as opposed to judgment, must be the rule for social engagement in congregations. Turning away from judgment, while turning toward the virtues of mercy, love, respect, and dignity, changes the way we are of service in the world.

When congregation members take part in social engagement, their self-understanding and perspective on the world changes in deep and lasting ways. First, people experience transformation when they have personal interaction with those that

6 Peter Buffett, "The Charitable-Industrial Complex," *New York Times*, July 7, 2013, http://www.nytimes.com/2013/07/27/opinion/the-charitable-industrial-complex. html?_r=0 (accessed March 26, 2014).

they serve. Second, having an opportunity to reflect with others on their experiences of service is powerfully transformative. Without personal relationship and some kind of ongoing reflective process, people are less likely to experience long-term transformation. The influence of relationship and reflection changes people's sense of mutuality with others and makes them more generous and likely to take on social service. This also makes people less comfortable returning to old attitudes and practices.

We find that there are many opportunities to reflect on our experiences. Sermon sharing—the work the people take on in completing the preachers' sermons—is one way. In sermon sharing, we always ask people to share their experiences, not their opinions. It is the lived experiences of each member that carry the wisdom of God, the presence of God that each of us encounters day-by-day in our lives. Opinions close down reflection from other people; opinions are like a line in the sand that you dare someone else to cross. Hearing others' experiences opens our imagination and wondering about our lives. This kind of work takes place in other places too: small groups, Godly Play classes, spiritual direction sessions, Bible study, and walks together at our parish retreat. The point is to keep the conversation going, not to imagine that there is an ending to it. God is speaking to each one of us, all the time; our job is to keep listening and share with others what we hear.

The call of Jesus Christ to share in God's mission in the world is like the lipstick stain on the icon in my former parish. Once we take on the work of social engagement, once we join Christ in his ministry of reconciliation and peace, the stain lingers on our souls. Try as we might, we can't quite get rid of it. Social engagement is all about transformation, in the world and in our lives. Whether we recognize it or not, we are made a new people in Christ's resurrection. We become more familiar to ourselves as we follow his example, doing what he did, speaking what he said. Our desires begin to change; our priorities change. We become less concerned with fear and more concentrated on peace. And that kiss-stain just gets darker and darker, more and more and more permanent the more we take on the work of Christ in the world. When we act like Jesus, when we sneak into someone's life, stealing a kiss that will leave a mark, we find out what it means to become the risen Christ in the world; the one who holds everything in his hands.

chapter 3

Friendship: The One Thing Truly Worthwhile

At St. Gregory's there's a lot of emphasis on finding God through relationships, through the community, through the set of relationships one cultivates over time, that being in love is a complicated thing, and it doesn't mean that you feel happy about everybody all the time.

—Dan C.

A T THE TOP of the cupola, above our altar table, there is an inscription from Gregory of Nyssa's last work. On one side it is written in Greek, on the other in English. It's from *The Life of Moses*, a theological reflection on the relationship between Moses and God, and what it has to do with the human soul. The phrase is simple and permeates everything that we do as a congregation: "The one thing truly worthwhile is becoming God's friend." That theological phrase defines our life together, but there is something more. If a congregation can be defined by one of the four Gospels, then St. Gregory of Nyssa is defined by the fourth gospel. Every March, on our feast day, we hear these words from the fifteenth chapter of John, chanted in a beautiful, medieval tone: "This is my commandment, that you love one another as I have loved you. No one has greater love than this, to lay down one's life for one's friends. You are my friends if you do what I command you. I do not call you servants any longer, because the servant does not know what the master is doing; but I have called you friends, because I have made known to you everything that I have heard from my Father." I have few opportunities to lay down my life for anyone, so trying to imagine what that looks like, apart from some sort of martyrdom fantasy I might keep tucked into the back of my imagination, is a hard thing for me. It's easier for me to simply live as a friend. John's gospel comes to its perfection in Jesus's definition of us as his friends. This kind of friendship—gospel friendship—animates our congregation. Although living in friendship is pretty straightforward, it is sometimes complicated in our life, as it is in any congregation. Friendship means demands and accommodation; it means gentleness and toughness. When it veers towards toughness, friendship isn't always pretty.

I was walking my dog, Frankie, thinking about friendship. Frankie is a rescue dog, what's called an American Dingo. He is a scrounger, a pack-centered creature that wants to know everything going on in our neighborhood, with a mean-sounding bark but a friendly, wagging tail. When he walks, he sniffs the ground for trash. At the park he ducks under bushes, looking for something repulsive to eat. We were in the park around the corner from our house. I looked away from Frankie for a moment and heard the unmistakable crunching sound he makes when he finds something truly despicable to eat. And I did what you do when you don't want your dog to eat filth; I pried his mouth open and stuck my hand inside to find a part of a dead bird. I probed his mouth, trying to get out the sharp-edged bones that can get caught in a dog's throat or tear up his gut. I scooped bones and greasy feathers out of his mouth. And he looked at me with that heartbreaking look of fear and disappointment, the look that makes me feel like the very worst pet owner in the world. I looked around the park to see if anyone had noticed, but there was no one around to see the full extent of my love for Frankie. Showing love to my dog isn't always pretty.

Living in friendship with other people is the same: sometimes it means digging through what repels us in order to bring healing and wholeness. When it comes to Frankie, it's pretty simple to live out of the virtues of gospel friendship. His affection is uncomplicated and essential. But pulling bones out of a wild dog's mouth is easy compared with being a loving friend to my human companions. Being a friend is messy and dangerous, along with being gorgeous and exhilarating. Gospel friendship is based on love, the kind of love that creates a permanent wound in your soul that is the source of both pain and life. It is more than a theoretical position; it's more than a top-ten list of do's and don'ts. Gospel friendship means surrendering a part of my will, a part of my desperate addiction to control, to another person. Gospel friendship means that my story and my future are not all about me; they're as much about the people I bind myself to in the community of faith. The great gift of congregational life is that anyone can come and be a part. Which also means that the other person may not be the most loveable sort of person; sometimes the person that I am called to befriend is the person that reason tells me to repel.

Jesus tells his disciples that gospel friendship is about obedience to his love. When it comes to gospel friendship, we have to discern the differences between the kind of obedience that Jesus gives us and the kind of obedience that destroys us. There are people who quote the Scriptures quite freely, calling others to surrender to abuse and domination. We can't live with that kind of bad news. Jesus's gospel friendship means that we have to listen to what the other person brings, and we have to discern how we will relate to that person. The tricky part is that sometimes gospel friendship looks pretty awful. My friend asks what I'd do: she wants to tell her husband that if she doesn't stop drinking, he'll take the kids and leave. Another friend tells me that my thoughtless words hurt her when all she really wanted was my support. In all the difficult places that friendship leads us, we have to be willing to press through our discomfort to the place where we are changed. We have to be obedient to Jesus's way of love, without seeking shortcuts. Gospel friendship is not for the faint of heart, but it changes everything.

Most translations of John 15 include these words: "This is my commandment: love one another as I have loved you," which is a beautifully vague thing to say. A better translation of the verse makes clear that the commandment isn't to love; the commandment *results* in love: "This is my commandment, so that you love one another as I have loved you." You will find the commandment's definition in Chapter 13: "If I, your Lord and Teacher, have washed your feet, you also ought to wash one another's feet. For I have set you an example, that you also should do as I have done to you." In order to love one another, we must serve one another. Jesus commands his disciples to bow down to each other, to humble themselves before each other; he commands us to do the same. It is in service that we learn how to love each other. It is in bowing down that we can take up love. This is the definition of gospel friendship.

Obedience to Jesus's commandment to serve requires our vulnerability to that wound I mentioned earlier, the wound that is created from love; the wound from which comes both pain and life. Gospel friendship makes you vulnerable; it means opening yourself to the other person. Gospel friendship opens you to the truth of yourself: it is in serving another, and loving that person, that your life increases. That's what it means to lay down your life for your friend. It means opening yourself to the love—and the pain—of being in relationship to another. It means gaining new life, by giving away our lives. It means being transformed by our willingness to live in friendship.

Laying down your life for another would be an easy thing if it only meant promising you'd die for someone. It's like the parent who tells his son, "I love you so much that if you were lying on a train track and a locomotive was coming toward you, I'd sweep you off the track and take your place." That's an easy enough pledge to make, because how often is that likely to happen? Let's make the scene really hard. What about placing your beloved before your career? What about losing face with your coworkers for the sake of your beloved? What about naming your beloved's addiction to his face? What about changing your carefully planned life to make room for your beloved when she becomes physically challenged? The list could go on. But my point is that gospel friendship only matters if it takes place in real situations in real life—not unimaginable places in an imaginary life. And the only way to get to the point where you can love so authentically is by practicing gospel friendship. This is why gospel friendship is such a powerful force for transformation in congregational life. Sharing real relationships changes people. Living in gospel friendship creates more capacity to serve and love the other. It brings the kind of vulnerability that makes us real, and ultimately more capable of knowing God.

❧

Once every six weeks or so, I choose not to assign myself to one of the Sunday morning services. On those rare Sundays, I don't have to preach or preside. I don't have to do the work of the liturgical deacon or wrangle liturgical lay leaders. All that I have to do is welcome people who come to worship with us. The first thing visitors find when they come to St. Gregory's on a Sunday morning is someone standing outside, handing out music books on the front steps of the church. On Sundays when I don't have a particular role in the liturgy, I take a turn handing out music books. This is the front line of welcoming visitors, and I try to do it with the same enthusiasm and commitment as do the regular volunteers who do this work. Because we value friendship as an expression of God's presence in our lives, we put a lot of energy into this kind of welcome.

The hard part is that, sometimes, we just want to hide. Of course, we don't call it hiding—we call it catching up with friends, or checking up on so-and-so. Sundays are prime time for congregations; it's the best time to nurture friendships that we enjoy with other parishioners. Almost every Sunday, I find myself in this bind: I want to talk to the people that I already know, those who are already my friends, but I see first-time visitors hanging around the edges. If I'm honest with myself, there are days when it's easier for me to talk to people who are already my friends and hide from people I don't know. But the commitment that I have made to looking for friendship in those I do not already know moves me out of the comfortable place of spending time with known friends. And so, I turn to the one I do not know and seek the image of God that they bear.

Living in gospel friendship is a decision that congregations have to make every day. At St. Gregory's, we strive to treat strangers as if they are already "insiders" in the congregation. Over the years, we have found that welcoming everyone with the same intention increases our sense of living in gospel friendship. In each of the three synoptic Gospels, you can read the story of Jesus returning to his hometown and being rejected by those who know him best. Luke's gospel is the most dramatic; the crowd drags Jesus to the edge of town to throw him off a cliff. In each of these stories there is a whiff of "Who do you think you are? We know you! We know where you come from!" Jesus's home folk don't know him at all. Like us they just know what they know from their own prejudgments. Jesus goes to his hometown and is rejected because he has become a stranger. He appears again and again as a stranger to those he meets along the way. We strive to see God's image in those we do not already know, in the strangers who come to us. We offer strangers a preferential welcome because we want to know more of God.

Relationships with strangers are built from this basic understanding. We want newcomers to participate in the liturgy and community life of the parish as much as they want. We become friends with strangers by sharing whatever it is that makes our congregation distinct, and listening to the new thing they are bringing to us. We are grateful to receive what strangers bring to us and ready to learn more about the ways that God is at work transforming both their lives and ours. This give-and-take works to make a lively community, one where we are all looking for new expressions of God's Spirit in our midst.

In congregational life, friendship operates in a very specific way; it is not like friendships that are only based on personal affinity. Like standing outside the church, welcoming visitors, friendship is first about presence. Our presence with strangers is based on the assumption that they too are friends of God. Friendship with God is the primary basis for living in relationship with everyone else in the congregation, as well as the world outside the congregation. Friendship with God acknowledges us as equals in relationship. If God is the first friendship to which we are invited, then we don't have to grasp jealously after the other person. Obviously, there are some people in the congregation that I like more than others, but that cannot be the criteria for choosing to live in relationship with people.

If friendship with God is the basis of the friendships we enjoy with other people, then we don't have to fake it in our friendships with others in the congregation. We don't have to hide behind a mask of being a perfect person as if our friendliness was the sole basis for friendship. We can choose to live in friendship on the basis of God's unconditional love and acceptance, and Christ's choice to call us friends. If friendship doesn't begin in the human-divine relationship, it will quickly devolve into friendship based on affinity or expediency. But it is God who chooses to call each one of us friends. That is the way that Jesus Christ reveals God to us. Only when we recognize that God calls us friends can we claim friendship with the other person.

Jesus's call to friendship depends on our commitment to being authentically ourselves. We have to be real to be friends. We won't be able to enter into real friendship with anyone if we believe that our friendship with God is built on a carefully constructed, false identity. Congregations must help their members to find ways to be healed of this burden. Otherwise, people will attempt to build friendship by what is not real. Instead of building friendship out of God's abundance, we will build friendship from our finitude. This is why we establish rules about those we can and cannot be friends with: Don't be his friend because he's too . . . Don't be her friend because I don't think I can bear her . . . That one is too different, that one is too much like my mother, that one is too inconvenient. The drive to segregate people, to alienate people because of their differences, perpetuates the brokenness of life that Christ came to restore. God's friendship is revealed in the friendships we share with people both like and unlike us. This is the template upon which the church is built.

The friendship to which Christ calls his followers seeks the well-being of the other person, even when it is costly. It is by serving each other that we learn how to live in love. The choice of the congregation is whether or not we will live in obedience to the call of God to live in friendship. We can ignore the call to friendship, but that choice will not lead to transformation. The decision to love, the decision to live in friendship with others, is what influences transformation.

✂

Ginny came to St. Gregory's, in part, to overcome years of homelessness, mental illness, alcoholism, and despair. Ginny, a gruff, raspy-voiced lesbian in her seventies, is an amazing part of our life together, and she is as unlike me as any person can be. "Hey, big guy!" she calls out to me as I approach the church. She sits in her wheelchair under the plum tree by the front doors, smoking her discount cigarettes, "Let me ask you about something." Although she had spent many years in unbearably painful situations, Ginny never gave up. She's a fighter, tough as nails. When she began to complain about having low energy, it never occurred to me that she was seriously ill. But when, after a lot of cajoling and bargaining she went to the doctor, she was diagnosed with cancer. She got weaker, rarely leaving her room at the single-room occupancy hotel where she lived in San Francisco's Tenderloin, except to come to church. Eventually, she couldn't manage her illness alone, something that Ginny had always done before. After a lot of phone calls and maneuvering, we found her a bed at the Zen Hospice. At first, Ginny hated it. "Look at this shit hole!" she would scream as I looked over the beautiful old Victorian mansion that the San Francisco Zen Center had dedicated to caring for those close to death. Ginny never lost her ability to complain.

I would visit Ginny at the Zen Hospice every other week or so. By this time we had mobilized an entire care team to visit, sitting with Ginny and talking. She spent a good part of the day on the back patio, smoking. When I visited her, I would occasionally join her in a smoke. We would talk about theology, and dying, and art, and her life. The conversations were sometimes difficult. Ginny is very hard of hearing and the cheap hearing aids she'd used for years had given out. I'd have to raise my voice to the point I worried that I was disrupting the peace and tranquility of the dying residents. I wasn't sure what the karmic burden of yelling at the Zen Hospice was, but it seemed like the wrong thing to do.

The challenge that we faced with Ginny was getting her a pair of hearing aids that would allow her to hear conversations more clearly. But Ginny was dying. She had no private insurance, and the public assistance that she received meant hearing aids would take months to get. By that time, Ginny would most likely be dead. One of the social workers at the hospice suggested buying Ginny hearing aids without insurance. It seemed like an extravagance, paying cash for something that a dying woman might only be able to use for a few weeks. "We can raise the money for hearing aids," I said to Sara, "It'll be the best $2,500 we ever spent." Like the ointment that Mary poured on Jesus's feet, another expensive extravagance, we decided to buy. Ginny hearing aids. It was a small act of gospel friendship.

The next week, Sara and I visited Ginny. Sitting in the patio at the Zen Hospice, I told Ginny that we would be able to get her hearing aids. "It's not that much money, and I'm sure people will be glad to contribute." She stared at me, eyes filling with tears, and pressed her cheek against my hand. "I never thought I could love a man as much as I love you, big guy. Thank you." There was a time in my life that I would have steered clear of someone like Ginny; too much trouble, too many demands. But crossing over the boundaries that we all establish, in order to sanitize our relationships, has powerfully transformed me. I thought that I was the one extending the energy of friendship to Ginny; the truth was, her friendship has transformed my life. Crossing boundaries transforms relationships and congregations.

When the church emphasizes friendship as a phenomenon that is based on God's choice to befriend each of us, instead of our personal affinity, we have the opportunity to practice conscious appreciation of people we might otherwise ignore. The choice to nurture friendships with people we have little personal affinity with expands our self-understanding and the meaning of being in community. Brian says of those who are unlike him, "No matter whether we see eye to eye or not, we still want you to be a part of the community. We still need you here."

Friendship is a major topic of conversation at St. Gregory's. People tell me that sharing friendship with each other changes them. They tell me that the friendships they have in the congregation are unique from those they experience in their lives outside of the church. Brian says, "Going to St. Gregory's forces me to have friendship with people that I wouldn't necessarily spend any time with." One of the only places where you have a chance of being in a relationship with people that are unlike you is in the church. This is the strength of the church today. Brian says, "I love the community because it forces me to interact with people that I wouldn't necessarily. And so I don't lose touch with humanity." Friendship leads us to a deepened sense of our essential nature as followers of Jesus Christ. Gospel friendship means choosing to engage other people, supporting them, and advocating for their well-being. It also means being open to the possibility of being changed as a result of the relationship.

Friendships that cross social boundaries powerfully influence the process of transformation in congregational life. At St. Gregory's, friendship is shared between those who might naturally be attracted to one another as well as between those who find little in common. Friendship is found across a spectrum that includes social, economic, racial, ethnic, gender, sexual orientation, and age differences. Crossing social boundaries to form friendships is a distinct opportunity the church possesses that is not always put into action. Betsy notes, "You know, a lot of churches want families. I am not a family. They say, 'Oh, gray-haired people!' You know, it's supposed to be a lifelong commitment, so you stay when you have gray hair."

Some congregations seek to enforce social boundaries. In these congregations, every demographic has its own subgroup: men, women, young adults, and so forth. Not long ago two women visited us and asked about special programs that we offer for LGBTQ people. I didn't have much to offer, "We're all just kind of together here—which is a pretty queer kind of thing."

One of the great benefits of mixing friendships across boundaries is that it changes the ways that people relate to everyone in the congregation. Brian says, "There are people at St. Gregory's that I get really excited about seeing. There are those at St. Gregory's that I think, 'Oh no, here we go again, we're going to get this long diatribe.' But it forces me to sit down and appreciate them." Developing a habit of engagement with people that we are not naturally attracted to makes us more resilient, flexible, and loving.

✄

The longer we remain in relationship with other people, the more deeply we can grow together in friendship. Although this is a benefit when it comes to the process of transformation, it is sometimes costly; it is costly and beautiful.

It's usually the last thing in the world I expect when my cell phone rings, to hear that a friend has died. When I answered the phone and heard the words on the other end, I had trouble making sense of what was said. "It's Felipe. He died last night." It didn't make sense. I had seen him the Sunday before, laughing after church, getting into his yellow VW and waving goodbye as he and his husband Otis drove away. I had that familiar, sickening feeling of things being just not right. The orderly progression of life had been disordered. Felipe was always smiling, always laughing, always alive. When he came to church on a Sunday, he would always call me Pablito and grab me and kiss me on the mouth. So when I got the call that he had died unexpectedly in his sleep, I felt that sinking feeling you get in your stomach and your soul. If you can't count on your friends staying alive, what can you count on?

I arrived at their house later that day. Otis was keeping vigil with a small group of friends. I walked into the house, and the first thing I noticed was the smell of burning frankincense. The odor of sanctity. The scent of Wisdom. I walked back to the bedroom where Felipe's body was resting. They had lovingly washed his body and dressed it in a white alb. They had tucked him into bed, like a sleeping child. He was surrounded by white flowers—a rosary and cross in his hands. "I was supposed to die first," Otis told me. Felipe was younger than Otis, seemingly in better health. "I heard him groan in the night, but didn't think about it. When I woke up, he was dead." Otis paused, "He went to sleep, and woke up asleep in the Lord."

We sat with him and told stories about Felipe. It was a group of friends remembering their beloved who had left them, even though his body rested next to us. We prayed. We all gathered around Otis. I took his hand in mine. We prayed about the pain of loss and the promise of comfort. We gave thanks to God for the bonds that tied us together eternally. God's Holy Wisdom was there. From the downward spiral of despair, I felt lifted to Wisdom's presence and knew that all things would work for good. The thing is, I didn't know how it would work for good—I still don't—but there was that presence, that order, that glimmering something more.

The thing about sitting with the dead body of a friend is that it is both familiar and unfamiliar. On the one hand, it is the same body that would reach out to embrace me, holding me closely, saying my name and sharing the peace of Jesus with me. On the other hand, it was still and cold. Otis kept Felipe's body at home until it was taken to the crematorium. In addition to the white alb and the flowers, his friends had packed bags of ice around his body. And I kept wondering fearfully if it would be enough to keep the body from decaying. Even twenty-four hours can change a dead body for the unthinkably worse. When I touched Felipe's hand, it was, literally, as cold as ice.

The next day I met everyone at the crematorium. It was a beautiful place, up in the hills of Marin County. The wind off the Bay blew softly. I went into the building, calm and well designed. It looked like the kind of place you'd host a tasteful cocktail party. But behind the wide door, toward the back of the building, was a plain, industrial space for cremation. Felipe's body was in a cardboard box on a gurney facing the heavy metal doors of a machine built for burning up bodies. Even with the door latched it made a sort of rushing noise. Otis had brought a beautiful red cloth to cover the cardboard casket. He also brought chunks of spicy smelling copal incense, rose petals, and lavender branches. We gathered with Otis around the cardboard box. And just as his friends had lovingly washed Felipe's body and dressed it in a white robe, now they tenderly covered the box with the sweet smelling gifts. I read the prayers for the assembly, including Felipe: "Acknowledge, O Lord, a sheep of thine own fold, a lamb of thine own flock, a sinner of thine own redeeming." When we had finished surrounding Felipe's body with as much love as we could, two workmen came forward and lifted the heavy metal door. The rushing noise increased. They carefully lifted one end of the cardboard box onto a roller at the entrance of the furnace and pushed in the box. The door slammed shut. We stood in silence for a moment and then embraced each other. As I put my arms around Otis, I softly repeated the words that we say every Easter: "Christ is Risen!" and he responded, "He is risen indeed!"

The enduring quality of friendship, the way that friendship deepens and changes over months and years, is transformative. Our congregation's choice to emphasize friendship as both a theological goal and an organizing principle is not the easiest way of constituting a congregation, but it is beautiful and nurtures transformation in people's lives. Congregations have to think about transformation over the long term. Gospel friendship must be our normative pattern of behavior over the long term. This is how congregations gain a deeper sense of inclusion and love. Connection is transformative, even when it is painful.

Friendship is not always easy. Since the friendship that

Jesus commands his disciples is not based on affinity or pref-
erence, congregations are composed of friends that might not
be our first choice of companions. We do not get to choose the
friends we will have in congregational life; God chooses our
friends for us. Margaret is a wise, canny woman who left her
belief behind years ago, yet remains a part of the congregation because of the way that it continues to fill her life. She has
taught Sunday school, served on the vestry, organized Easter,
and drives Esther—our eldest parishioner, now 101 years old—
to church every Sunday. Margaret has found that her years at
St. Gregory's have given her the ability to love others genuinely:
"I'm very comfortable with the people here and have actually
learned over the years to become a great deal more genuinely
tolerant of people who annoy the shit out of me." Despite the
annoyance that relationships bring, Margaret has committed
herself to friendship in the community. Living in friendship
teaches us how to become better friends to those we would
not have chosen. Rather than waiting until she experiences an
ideal relationship with other members, Margaret has decided
to maintain friendships with those she finds difficult. Tolerance
for others is quite different from love for others, and Margaret
explicitly chooses love. Friendship has the potential to prepare
people to live differently in the world.

✻

Paul writes these words in his Letter to the Romans: "Now
hope that is seen is not hope. For who hopes for what is seen? But
if we hope for what we do not see, we wait for it with patience."
Hope is at the heart of friendship.

There was a terrible accident at the end of my block one
Friday morning. As I was backing my car out of the garage,
checking to see if there were any other cars coming down the
street, I heard a crash. I turned in the direction of the sound
and saw an SUV rolling over, in mid-air. I grabbed my phone

to call 911, got out of the car, and rushed toward the car that the SUV had hit, causing it to roll over. The car's front end was smashed, and the driver's-side door was partly open. The woman inside the car was screaming for someone to get her out. Steam or smoke was coming out of the car, probably from the exploded airbags, but it could have been something smoldering inside. It was frightening to imagine a car on fire at the end of my block. My neighbor, Mike, had come out of his house, and the two of us ran up to the car, as well as two construction workers from the apartment project being built down the next block. Mike is a good guy, a tech worker who rides his bike everywhere. He's cool headed, the kind of man you want around in a crisis. The four of us pried the door open and got the woman out. I was surprised at the sound of bent metal on twisted metal as we worked the door open. Broken glass was under my feet, and some sort of liquid began to puddle nearby.

Amazingly, the woman in the car was not injured—just really freaked out. I gently grabbed hold of her arm, put my other hand on her shoulder, and walked her to the sidewalk. Slowly, I helped her to sit down on the curb. I knelt by her and put my hand on her back, trying to calm her. It was the same gesture that my father would make when I was restless in bed as a little boy. It was a kind of prayer, hoping that she was not injured, that she was going to be all right. She kept repeating, "He ran the red light!" I looked over at the SUV, which had rolled all the way back onto its wheels and thought, "I hope that guy is alive." I didn't say much to the woman. I simply held the palm of my hand against her back as she trembled.

In the midst of terrible events, we hope. But we also hope in the midst of ordinary events. And in the course of a day, terrible events and ordinary events merge. We hope for our children's futures. We hope that our jobs will last. We hope that our friends won't let us down. We hope we win the lottery. We hope a lot. And sometimes it seems that I don't even know what I mean when I say the word hope. Hope is not a romantic notion;

it is a tough, scrappy thing. Hope is a function of struggle; it is what is built in us when we strive to do hard, scary things. Hope is not so much an emotion as it is a behavior. Hope comes when people set goals, pursue them tenaciously and with real perseverance, and believe they have the ability to achieve them. Hope is not how we feel; it is how we think. Hope means learning to deal with disappointment. Hope needs determination. Hope grows as we make an attempt, fail, and try again. Hope requires us to practice compassion. Hope is not a gauzy feeling that things will somehow work out for us. Hope is about struggle. And hope is about relationships. Hope is what makes friendships last over the long term.

Not long after we got the woman to the sidewalk, I heard the sirens as the ambulance came. I asked the woman if she had any pain in her back, or neck, or arms or legs. She said she didn't, just her chest that had been hit by the airbags. I said, "The ambulance will be her soon, just in case." The paramedics arrived and took over. I removed my hand from my anonymous friend's back and stood up. I looked over at the SUV. It hardly looked like it had been in a wreck, even though it had flipped over in the crosswalk. The crosswalk where, twenty seconds before, a woman on her way to work had crossed the street. I was frankly as angry at the guy driving the SUV as I was worried about his condition. People speed down that street all the time, trying to make it through the intersection, even as the lights change from green to yellow to red. The SUV could have slammed into the building next door to mine and killed my neighbor's baby who slept in the corner room on the ground floor. The SUV could have rolled over the woman who crossed the street, or the father pushing his child in a stroller who had crossed a moment before. I remember thinking, "I hope that guy is okay, and I hope those idiots stop speeding down my street, putting us all in danger."

Even though she seemed to be all right, the paramedics took the woman whose car was smashed to the hospital for a checkup.

The strangely intimate moment of my caring for her was over; she didn't even look my way as they led her to the ambulance. I returned to my car and began the drive to St. Gregory's. As I drove away from the wreck, I remember thinking to pray for the guy in the SUV. I don't know what happened to him. What I know without a doubt is that the Spirit who prays continually for me prays continually for him, and for the woman who sat on the sidewalk, for my neighbor, Mike, and the construction workers who got her out of the car, for the paramedics who would spend the rest of the day caring for the maimed and injured, for the woman who crossed the street just a few seconds before the accident and the father pushing his stroller. In the midst of the struggles of this life, that prayer continues. And it builds up hope in all of us.

Fundamentally, hope is relational. Hope means personal allegiance and abiding confidence in another person. When I tell my husband, Grant, that I hope he has a good day, particularly if the previous day hasn't been good, I mean that I believe in him and his abilities to make it through his struggle. I believe that there is a pattern in our lives that leads toward wholeness and peace. When I tell a sick friend, I hope she gets better, I mean that I will be there for her if she doesn't get better. When I look hopefully on the children of my congregation, I mean that I will do whatever I can to help them to grow to be strong in the face of their struggles without getting in the way of their failures. Hope is a force that holds us together. We do not hope alone. We look to each other and respond to the needs that we all experience. Hope binds us together in our communities. Hope makes us the Body of Christ. This is a work of the Holy Spirit. And, as the church, it is our life's work.

This doesn't mean that we can stop striving in our relationships; that we'll never have to struggle as friends. If it's true that struggle builds hope in us, then we need to struggle in our relationships, our ministries, and our engagement with the world. We need to struggle because it is only in the struggle that we learn how to hope. It is only as we care enough to struggle in relationships that are not easy that we have a hope of growing in friendship. God knows our struggle. And God knows that it is a hard struggle as we grow in friendship with each other.

The Holy Spirit is always with us, even though we may not perceive her presence. She is at prayer for us all—individually and as the Body of Christ. Her prayer is as deep as a mother's groaning for her children, as constant as a wind blowing the mist away. And like that wind, we cannot know where she is coming from or where she is going. In our lives all that we can do is pay attention, look around at the world God loves, struggle to show up, and do what we can. This is how we can persevere as hope is built in us, and as we use that hope in forging friend-ships with others.

There comes a time in a relationship where the hard thing to do becomes the thing that we must do, if we are becoming more real in our lives. It's a kind of healing. It's that place where we step out from what we have known in the past to a new kind of life in a world that we do not know. It's a healing of our desire for the other which looks like responding out of love instead of fear. So the question becomes not, "Am I good enough to be your friend?" The question becomes, "How is my relationship with God bound up in my friendship with you?" Jesus doesn't love me because I'm loveable. Jesus loves on the basis of his love of the Father. Jesus doesn't call us his friends because he needs more friends; he calls us friends because he wants our lives to be full. It isn't just a neat idea to abide in God's love; it is the only way that we can be saved from a culture that believes more in control than blessing. Living in friendship with God and one another is the only way our desire can be healed; turned from self-serving to other-serving. It's the only way that we can move from just thinking about God to admitting our soul's depen-dence on God. And it's the only way that we can do that thing that the gospel tells us about—and that Gregory of Nyssa called true perfection—becoming God's friend.

Two weeks after the SUV hit the car at the end of my block, I was presiding in the liturgy at St. Gregory's. It was midway through the service, following the prayers, when I go to the far end of the building to meet the children who bring the gifts of bread and wine to the altar in the center of the room. As I walked toward the rotunda, I saw a woman and child standing just inside the door. She was carrying a potted plant in one hand and holding her son's hand with the other. At first, I didn't recognize her, but then her face became clear to me: it was the woman who had been in the accident. I found out later that a member of St. Gregory's had been on her way to work with this woman's mother, and they had been stuck in the traffic caused by the accident. My friend had heard me talking about the accident, put two and two together, and got word to the woman that I was a priest at St. Gregory's. "I should have known you were a minister," she said, "you were so loving to me after the accident." She handed me the plant— "a thank you gift," she explained—and turned to leave. "Why don't you stay for the rest of the service?" I quickly asked her. "No. Church really isn't my thing. But thank you. Thank you." A stranger had become a friend. The bond of friendship that Jesus commanded his disciples had been forged between us. Church wasn't her thing, but the love of God between us was strong enough to make something new, something real, in our relationship. That, at least, is my hope.

✄

Friendship in congregational life affects the process of transformation in three ways. First, sharing friendship over the long term adds a sense of stability in our lives, something that is often missing in other areas of people's lives. Next, seeking friendships that cross social boundaries allows us to engage those with whom we would have little chance of interacting. Crossing social boundaries leads to a broader experience of relationship. Finally, friendship provides a context within which to practice relational skills that can be applied in other areas of our lives. Practicing friendship influences the ways that we respond to others outside of the congregation. In particular, practicing friendship within the congregation teaches us how to restore relationships that have been broken.

A few years ago I was having lunch the Wednesday of Holy Week at a sushi restaurant not far from the church. It was packed. Sara and I got a table next to a couple and their small, red-headed baby. The baby was mostly quiet, but like everyone who sits next to a baby in a restaurant I thought, "just my luck." Sara and I had been working on preparations for Good Friday and Easter liturgies, wrestling with the texts that we would be preaching, worrying about the last-minute things that needed to get done. We needed food and peace and quiet, and wound up sitting next to this baby.

Sara asked a question that I've heard on other Good Fridays in other churches: "Why do you think that people like Good Friday more than Easter?" It's a fair question. People like both, but for many it is just easier to relate to Good Friday. "Maybe it's because people know what it's like when someone dies, but someone rising from the dead—that's just different." I wondered about the question and looked at the little red-headed baby.

Jesus's death on the cross is something that looks very human. Many of us have lived with friends who suffer and die; few of us are responsible for the death of a friend. But I think it's fair to say that all of us have sacrificed a friend for the sake of some other goal. Jesus's death on the cross shows us something about this sacrificial impulse: it is never the final word. The cross shows how humans use violence to sanctify our bad choices. But the resurrection is all about God's power poured out everywhere, including our bad choices. The cross shows us what we know about ourselves: we sacrifice those we love. The resurrection tells us we have to tear up our plans, accept forgiveness for our bad choices, and begin again. The resurrection is all about transformation.

I looked over at the little red-headed baby. His mother had him on her breast, feeding and soothing him. But he was clearly old enough for solid food. So he went back into his little highchair. The mother kept giving him things to eat, little bits of rice and tofu. The mother would place the food in front of him, and the baby would play with the food and then put it in his mouth.

The waiter brought us our lunch, and I began to dig into it; eating the way you do when you've skipped breakfast and have been working hard all morning. I went from one square of the bento box to the next, loving the way the food tasted, the way it filled my mouth with pleasure and my stomach with satisfaction. I looked over at the little red-headed baby. Every time his mother would lean over and put some more food in front of him, he would take it and stuff it in his mouth. He would laugh with delight. He would raise his face up to his mother, mouth wide open, begging her to feed him more. More rice, more tofu. Feed me. Watch me smile. Hear me laugh. It was a revelation, this baby's laughter. He was noisy and funny. He was alive and mysterious and so full of honesty and joy that I saw something I hadn't expected to see over my lunch. I saw something that my theological speculation couldn't deliver. The little red-headed baby looked like the resurrection: so full of pleasure and delight and life. He looked like Jesus, stepping out of his tomb and breathing in the wet, cool, morning air.

We have to start paying closer attention to the power of the resurrection when it is revealed to us in random, everyday moments in life. Like a baby raising his face to his mother in delight, we can see the power of the resurrection rising up around and within us. That power means that when our friendships are broken by betrayal or indifference, we can trust in the new life that God plants in us. It might be inconvenient. It might make you odd. It might make you tear up your plans and start your life anew. But the life that Jesus brings from his tomb will fill you with the power to remake what has been broken in us. Then you will discover that your friendships are full of passion and power and forgiveness and beauty and freedom. Then you will find the power of friendship to fully, beautifully transform your life.

The founding document of St. Gregory's, written by Richard Fabian in 1978, contains these words: "From the beginning God made people to share his own life of love, and in living that life together to find their true selves, and his purpose for them. This common life changes form with times and places, but it is one life, because God wishes people of all times and places to become one in him." All of the ways that St. Gregory's has taught me about transformation, all the people with whom I share transformative relationships, all the challenges and joys of our shared life come down to these words. God has created us to live together in love, to find our true identities in that love, and to discover our purposes in life through that love. God is calling us all to a new kind of life—a life lived in friendship with others. This new life is defined for us in Jesus's resurrection from the dead; this is the source of our transformation.

In the following chapters, we will explore the ways that transformation works in congregational life. We will look at the kinds of things that congregations do as a regular part of their shared life, and discover the power of transformation that is within these common things.

chapter 4

Worship: Speaking the Truth to God

*What swung it for me convincingly was
that at St. Gregory's, God has more
elbow room than I have ever experienced
God having in my life. I found that
God just had more ways to reach me.
From the side and from the front.
The music, the preaching, the
community, the feast of the senses.*

—Mark L.

EVERYTHING THAT I know about God has passed through my mouth. In my infancy, the mediatrix of God's grace was my mother's breast. From her body she gave me life, and then—from her body—she gave me what I needed to stay alive, to grow, to become, and to know God. Later there were other foods, other bodies, other means of staying alive, growing, becoming, and knowing God. Of all the food that has passed into my mouth and become me, the most significant has been the bread and wine that are Christ's Body and Blood. The chalice of wine—or in my earlier life in another denomination, the little plastic shot glass of grape juice—took the place of my mother's breast. The paten of bread—or brass tray of desiccated matzo earlier in life—took the place of the meals and bodies and bottles that could never quite fill my soul, although some came closer than others. It was that divine food—bread of heaven, blood of the New Covenant—that both became my body and moved my body further and further into the life of God. This life, which is the source of all lives, was what I wanted most. This food transformed my life.

But there is another reality that I have to face: I don't always want to be transformed by God. I don't want God's life upsetting the order of my life. Sometimes I want to be in charge, have opinions, care little, be numb. But my mouth, long accustomed to being fed what I need to live, always wants to return to the bread and wine. It's like my friend Mary Jo, who gets an idea of what she wants for dinner and describes the desire saying, "My mouth is shaped for shrimp, not steak." So my mouth is shaped to eat the food that nourishes me with the presence of God. I want that food in my mouth. The easy, terrible grace of God, the extravagant, succulent mercy of God, the shattering, re-creative justice of God—all of these have come to me from the hand of a friend or a stranger into my mouth. In the language of the church, we call this gobbling up of God *Eucharist,* a word that means thanksgiving. It is the central action whereby we remember who we really, truly are.

The Eucharist is at the heart of worship. It is the action that has the power to transform every human life. The Eucharist is the Church's response to a world that doesn't seem to care whether or not we remember our true selves. To the contrary, too often the dominant cultures of this world seek to dismember human beings, their bodies, their loves, their desires, and their callings. William Cavanaugh writes in *Torture and Eucharist* of Chile during the dictatorship of Pinochet, a regime that regularly used torture as a way of social discipline. He claims that torture isolates people so that they can become useful to the dominant regime. Further, he claims that the Eucharist transforms people into the body of Christ, who always resists destructive power. Cavanaugh writes that "Torture creates victims; Eucharist creates witnesses." The Eucharist is the transformative practice that has the power to remake what human sin unmakes. Worship, with the Eucharist at its center, recreates, remakes, and remembers what is broken by the world's misuse of justice. Worship fuels transformation.

Eucharist is a way of seeing the world that has the power to remember the world from the imagination of God. It is real, and it makes us real. Eucharist gives a name and an identity to people who have no reason for being in communion with each other. As an old friend of mine used to say, the Eucharist confects reality.

I witness the transformational power of the Eucharist when we gather for worship at St. Gregory's, particularly in the lives of our children. When Soren first came to the church with his mother and two siblings, they were completely unfamiliar with what we were doing. Soren was seven years old. Since he didn't know the rules that subtly correct us in worship, he would sometimes interrupt the service. For example, I'd ask a rhetorical question in a sermon, and Soren would immediately call out his answer. When we move to the altar for Eucharist, I make sure that Soren stands as close to the table as he can, so that he can see and hear what we're doing. He takes this work seriously. As I stand and chant the ancient prayer over the bread and wine,

I look at Soren and see that he is quietly chanting along with me. Sometimes he looks up to the massive icon of dancing saints that line the walls. Who does he see? It is a moment that is so wrapped in mystery that trying to answer that question makes the wonder of it evaporate. I simply have to stand in that space, step out of the center of my life, and witness transformation in a boy's experience. Whenever people can step out of the center and begin to see the world from a new perspective, there is a moment of transformation. Worship gives people a vision of the world through a new optic: seeing the way that God does.

Episcopalians don't have a dogmatic system of belief or a shared confession of faith. Instead, we stake a huge claim on worship: it is the way that we learn who God is, who the other is, and what the world means. Too often we confuse this claim by paying too much attention to things like taste and class and politics and conventional ideas of beauty. These are the kinds of things that can make for a very toxic approach to worship.

Years ago I was serving communion at a former parish. The practice there was that worshipers would form lines and slowly walk up to an altar rail, kneeling on the worn, red velvet cushions. I'd give each a small round wafer of bread, then an assistant offered a silver chalice of sweet, red wine. People would hold their hands up to me, some looking at me, seeking some recognition. Others would avert their gaze to some point beyond the rear wall of the church, the place where their prayers were set. To each one I would say, "The Body of Christ, the Bread of heaven." I came to a mother and her young child. I said the formula and placed a wafer in the woman's upturned hands. Her daughter had raised her hands in the same way as her mother, so I began to place a wafer in her hands. Then it happened. The mother slapped her daughter's hands away. Confusion and pain flooded her eyes and mine, too. How could violence like this interrupt a moment of communion with God? I found out later that—as the mother said—her daughter didn't understand what Eucharist was all about, so she didn't want her to receive it. I tried, unsuccessfully I'm sure, to hide my anger when I said, "And I suppose that you understand all about it?" Without missing a beat, she replied, "Of course."

Episcopalians have strong opinions about their approach to the Eucharist, about who is worthy to receive it and who is not. These opinions are projected onto the stuff of the Eucharist: wafers vs. real bread, Rite I vs. Rite II, kneeling to receive vs. standing, and on and on. Many of these divisions focus energy on the place where we gather the bread and wine: the altar. The altar is a piece of furniture, sometimes made of wood, sometimes made of stone. Its purpose is to be the place where a priest takes bread and wine from the community, setting it apart with prayer and corporate intention, and returning it to the congregation as Christ's Body and Blood. Perhaps people's opinions settle so strongly on the altar because they believe it is the only meeting point between human and divine desire. But it's also the place from which the meal at the center of the Eucharist is served. In other words, it's a table. In too many places it exists behind a kind of spiritual velvet rope, close to the hungry but removed by idolatrous concerns about purity. I will always remember a woman in my former parish who asked if her sinfulness should keep her from touching the altar. I was dumbstruck by her question: if the sinful aren't the ones who most need to draw near to the altar, who can? Too often, our scrupulosity, our concern for purity, and our vexing opinions turn the Eucharist and the altar into symbols of exclusion and alienation.

The altar at the center of St. Gregory's worship is a semiround, wooden table. It is regularly used for blessing bread and wine, but it is also used for other things. I use it as a worktable sometimes. Other times we use it as the centerpiece for our weekly food pantry. After the service on Sundays, we put refreshments on it and keep the Eucharistic celebration going with coffee and tea. We can use the table this way because we are clear about what it is: when we vest it, covering it with a colorful cloth, it is the mystical meeting point between God and us. When we uncover it, it's the place where we swap stories or organize the choir folders. It's a functional table, on the same level as the people, not lifted up on a platform behind an altar rail. It is a place that is designed to include everyone. The table of the Eucharistic meal has to be one to which everyone is welcome, not just because we want to be inclusive but because we want to be made real.

The altar is the place where the distinction between "us" and "them" is not only irrelevant but also incorrect. Anything that obscures this reality is a problem precisely because it frustrates the intention of Jesus that everyone be fed right now without any preparation. Jesus welcomed the undeserving to his table. He violated the purity rules of who could be included and who had to be excluded. His profligate welcome ultimately resulted in betrayal and execution at the hands of the Empire. Eating with the right kind of people was religiously important in Jesus's day, but it was also politically important. There was a widely held opinion that God would not restore Israel unless the people were perfect, ritually pure. Jesus was deliberately impure in the way he shared the table with sinners. His actions encouraged others to eat with the wrong kinds of people. To his critics, this meant that Jesus was partially responsible for the Roman occupation of God's holy land. It wasn't just that he was flaunting the required purity rules; he was undermining his followers' devotion to them. When Jesus welcomed everyone to dine, it was something fundamentally subversive.

Jesus showed what God's Commonwealth was like by sharing the table with undeserving and unprepared people. Remembering these people, not only the righteous and the worthy, was the complete embodiment of his teaching. Everything that he did and said was charged with the same generosity and overwhelming love. This was not just a social innovation; it was the sign of God's presence in him, a presence that would not wait for us to get ready or clean up our messes. As St. Gregory's co-founder, Rick Fabian writes, "God is already here working with all of you; you have no time to prepare for, learn about, win, or manage God's coming; now you must respond; and your response today makes all the difference."[7] Which means that the presence at the altar of strangers, the unprepared, wicked people, and the undeserving is the surest sign of the real presence of Christ in the Eucharist. Instead of avoiding people who make me feel uncomfortable in worship, these are the ones who God sends to St. Gregory's to show us where she is already at work, making a new creation.

My husband hardly ever comes to worship at St. Gregory's, or anywhere else; he left Christianity behind years before we met. The exception is Christmas Eve; he always comes to the pageant service. He enjoys watching the children tell the story, each one wearing a costume made of old vestments and cast off caftans. But when it comes time for communion, he steps as far away from the altar as possible. "I'm a member of the heathen hubbies club," he explains to parishioners who try to draw him closer. As long as I've known him, he has refrained from taking the bread and wine. "I feel like a hypocrite," he explains. "Who doesn't," I reply. Sometimes the conversation ends there, other times I tell him, again, what receiving communion is about: welcoming everyone without exception. But he consistently chooses not to receive communion—except when he gets cornered.

When we first arrived at St. Gregory's, we were invited to a dinner that included Eucharist. This practice expanded from the way that we celebrate Eucharist on Maundy Thursday. We use a very ancient prayer for this service, based on an ancient source called the *Didache*. We place the Eucharist in the context of a dinner around tables. We share a meal and stories and bread and wine. For some people, this is the first opportunity to receive the invitation to communion. It is a real invitation, which means that some people choose not to take communion. So, when Grant and I were invited to a dinner at a parishioner's home, there was a Eucharist. There, in the middle of a perfectly

---

7 Richard Fabian, "First the Table, Then the Font," http://www.saintgregorys.org/uploads/2/4/2/6/24265184/firstthetable.pdf (accessed November 8, 2016).

good meal, a priest raised bread and wine, blessed and shared it around the table. Since we were seated around the table, Grant felt like he couldn't pass on receiving the bread and wine. He took communion, which both confounded and annoyed him.

After dinner as we were driving home, he turned to me and asked, "Do they have goddamn communion at every dinner party?" His response is the only natural one that I can think of for a man who was raised in an Episcopal church where communion was an event more about guarding the prepared against the unprepared. Grant's experience has shown him that the church is more about excommunication and exclusion than it is about fellowship and welcome. And I still invite him to come to the table, to receive the bread and wine, which are Christ's Body and Blood. I do this not because I worry that his choice not to receive somehow puts his soul in peril, but because I believe that it is precisely the person who has experienced exclusion who is essential to making the Eucharist real for those of us who believe we are insiders.

What the people of St. Gregory's have learned around the dining table, which is also the Eucharistic table, is not only the connection of the sacramental and ordinary, but the reality that God is pleased to be found in what is common. Unlike a dinner party where everyone is happily seated at table with friends, we take the same risk as Jesus who shared his last meal with friends who were also betrayers. The table of Jesus is not nice and safe; it is risky. The risk of inclusion is what makes us whole. We gather around the bread and wine to see that it is precisely in the common things of our lives that God is found. Even when eating the bread and wine causes scandal and confusion, God is present.

⁂

Worship is a bright light that shines on our experiences and shows how they are charged with divine energy. It also shines on our failings, illumining their need of divine transformation.

In theological terms, some of these points of contact between human experience and the divine are sacraments, ways in which everyday reality is enhanced, defined, and changed into eternal reality.

The sacraments, traditionally listed as Eucharist, Baptism, Confirmation, Penance, Anointing of the Sick, Matrimony, and Holy Orders, are the signs of God's grace revealed in Jesus Christ. The chief work of God in Christ is in reconciling all things to Godself through the cross. It is this work that the sacraments chiefly show to us. The liturgy is the place where we receive the good news of salvation through meal, bath, touch, and speech. God's grace transforms these common human actions, and God promises that these are moments in which transformation takes place. Everything that we bring to worship is touched by the power of God, transformed by sacramental grace, making us new.

My husband and I do not frequently worship together; our shared life in God is found outside of the church. So when I start talking about the power of worship to transform life, he gives me a skeptical look, a tilt of the head and squint of the eye. Sometimes he'll ask some variation of the question, "In a world full of hurt, is worship the best thing you have to offer?" It's a good question. Many churches construct an artificial dichotomy between the needs of the world and the worship of God—like it's just too messy to mix up the pain of the world and the artificial prettiness of worship. But I believe there is another way of looking at worship: it is an engine of transformation.

Everything that we do in worship comes from the everyday things of our lives, showing the ordinary to be filled with God's grace. The ancient symbols of worship relate to the most common events in life; they are for every longing soul. The Sacraments are about common life: the meal, the bath, the touch, and the speech. Because of this Eucharist, baptism, healing, corporate prayer, and preaching are familiar actions to strangers, children, the uninitiated, and the unprepared. The sacraments manifest the transforming love of God in every part of our lives: time, history, our stories, and our work.

Worship transforms time. Every Sunday is not merely the first day of the week; it is always the Day of Resurrection. Regardless of the season of the church year, every Sunday is the Easter Feast. Sunday is the day that the church gathers together for its common work of worship. We are revealed to be a new creation, not only those who work in offices or tech companies. On Sunday, each one of us is recognized as a member of the Royal Priesthood, a guest at the Messianic Banquet, a Prophet of the Most High. We look not only to the past and the present, but also to the future, and Christ's promise to abide with us forever. We claim the future as God's domain when we join the acclamation, "Christ has died, Christ is risen, Christ will come again."

Worship transforms history. The liturgy places a question mark over the assumption that history is either an ascent by human will or devolution into chaos. Liturgy—*leitourgia*—is two things at once: the common work of a group that is greater than could have been done by an individual, and the work of a few on behalf of the many. It is in the liturgy that we discern our call to live as Christ in the world. The liturgy is where we begin to take up God's ministry of reconciliation, changing the course of human history by the grace of God.

Worship transforms our stories. When the dominant text of the culture becomes one of oppression and exploitation, such as those texts that have sought to control queer people, women, and people of color, among others, worship serves as a place for telling the dangerous stories of salvation. By hearing the stories of redemption in the Hebrew Scriptures, the wonders and signs of the Kingdom wrought by Jesus in the Gospels, the non-compliance of the early church in the narrative of empire in the Epistles, we receive a counter-narrative of liberation. The repetition of sacred story as part of worship reinforces a new narrative in our imaginations. As these stories are heard season after season, year after year, they may become a part of our narrative.

Worship transforms our work. When we come to worship, we hear a new story, one that gives us work to take up in the world. Worship gives us permission to undermine every dominant system of oppression we may encounter. However, this is not a violent act that seeks to oppress the oppressor; the liturgy wants to work for the reconciliation of all people. Worship has the power to change us, to change the church and change society. This is why worship is beautiful: it has the power to create what we'd never known before, to open new vistas and new relationships.

�֍

We get a lot of visitors at St. Gregory's. Each week we expect about thirty percent of the congregation to be people who have never worshiped with us before. Some people come as spiritual tourists—folks who are looking for an experience that they can't quite name. Some who come are like me—church nerds who are hung up on the art of worship. These are the ones who usually have some training in how worship is supposed to work. They tend to cast a delighted gaze at what we're doing. But sometimes these visitors' gaze holds only criticism. One Sunday, just as the early service was about to begin, an older man came into the church with a young couple. I'd seen this configuration before: a parent comes to visit his children in San Francisco and insists that they go to the nearest Episcopal church. This particular man walked through the tall front doors of the building and just stopped. He looked up at the icon of dancing saints on the walls with something that looked like contempt. Scanning the room, his eyes were full of judgment. I walked toward him to greet him, and he looked at me with the same disdain. "This looks more like a mosque than a Christian church!" I resisted the urge to say that mosques don't usually have so many depictions of the human form. Knowing better, I let him turn and leave, his adult children apparently relieved at the opportunity to escape worship. Opinions about how worship is supposed to work are close to the hearts of many people. Their need to guard opinions keeps them from stepping away from the center and observing the potential of worship to change them.

There are times when we think knowing matters more than being transformed by our experiences. For some of us, it matters more that we light all the candles on the altar in the correct order than strive to live in love with our enemies. For others, it matters more that the behavior of children and other social outcasts is controlled than welcomed into the mystery of God. Maybe this is because it's just easier to pay attention to the details of worship than to the purpose of worship, which is to tear us out of our central location in the world and let God hold that space. When we occupy the center, it means we will count our own opinions, experiences, and prejudices as more significant than the mercy and power of God. When we occupy the center, it blinds us to where God is at work, striving to transform creation in love. All that we can see is our false selves, severed from the true self that rests in the heart of God. When we come to worship, stepping out of the center, we can begin to notice who God really is, who our neighbors truly are, and that each of us is infinitely loved. Worship makes us vulnerable in ways that are threatening to some, so threatening that it seems better to react violently and guard some sense of purity than it does to be transformed.

I keep an eye on visitors who come to worship. I like to see what is opening them up and what is confusing to them. If they have children, I pay attention to how they inhabit the space. Children are like the canary in the church's coal mine: If they get what we're doing, if they're relaxed and enjoying the experience, it means we're doing our job well. If children are paying attention in the service, it's a sure bet that their parents will be, too. The experience of worship is so important to us at St. Gregory's that everything we do in the liturgy we do for people who have never been with us before. It is our visitors' desire and hope that we pay attention to. When we do this, we know we're doing our job well. When I see that something has opened them up—a smile, a touch, uplifted eyes—I know that we have moved from doing worship correctly to letting God hold the center while we are at prayer. Welcoming those who have never had a place at the table is our way of living into Jesus's example and teaching, his life and his death.

Worship teaches people how to live together with each other and with God. After the liturgy, we invite everyone to sit with the preacher and debrief the experience. We call this time "Fifteen Good Minutes." People, both first-time visitors and members, ask all kinds of questions: about the sermon, about our ministries, about the way that we worship. For as long as I can remember, we have tried to steer people away from questions that are restatements of opinion toward questions about what they have experienced. More specifically, we ask the question, "What did you see?"

Randy, a schoolteacher without children of his own, notices what happens when children are invited into the center of worship. In the course of the liturgy one Sunday, Randy invented a liturgical job that he shares with a child. Before we hear the reading of Scripture, we sing and offer incense, amplifying our prayer and preparing us to listen. The container of incense sits on a stand next to a brass bowl that contains burning coals resting on a stone. The incense we use is a mixture of lavender flowers and benzoin resin; its smoke is less choking than incense made of frankincense. One Sunday the assigned leader in the service forgot to add the incense to the burning coals in the bowl by the lectern. Seeing an opportunity, Randy quickly walked up to the lectern with a child and held the bowl of burning coals so that the child could add incense. It was both an unplanned moment of beauty in the liturgy and an empowering use of worship to welcome a child into leadership. But it would not have happened if Randy hadn't been open to seeing what was happening in worship.

When we talk about what is happening in worship, we want people to step back from opinions and pay attention to their senses. People report what they have seen, heard, tasted, smelled, and felt. From this point, we can take their experiences and work together to talk about the theological purposes for why we do what we are doing. If we start with the theology, people's eyes sort of glaze over, so we try to locate theology in our senses and longing. We find that theology that doesn't begin in our bodies and our senses is not really worth the effort.

Good theology is an attempt to tell the story of human longing for God—and of God's promise that all of creation will be redeemed. As followers of Christ, we are claimed by a theology that makes God known through Jesus's teachings, actions, and life. And this always, inevitably, centers on his cross and resurrection, and their effect on us. What Christ accomplishes on the cross and in trampling down death in the resurrection shows the nature of God: one whose love has no boundaries and whose mercy is absolute, who welcomes everyone without exception. This is the whole point of worship: to manifest new life in the midst of a world of loss and struggle. In this reality, we are transformed.

Randy's experience, in crafting a new action in the liturgy, points out the importance of improvisation in worship. Improvisation is more than just filling in the missing pieces of some liturgical action; it adds something new to an original action. Improvisation is a welcome action that remakes what we had previously known. Keith Sawyer, a scholar of creativity, innovation, and learning, writes that improvisation must be contained: "All improvisers know that improvisation does not mean that anything goes; improvisation always occurs within a structure, and all improvisers draw on ready-mades—short motifs, or clichés—as they create their novel performance."[8]

---

8   R. Keith Sawyer, "Improvisation and the Creative Process: Dewey, Collingwood, and the Aesthetics of Spontaneity," *Journal of Aesthetics and Art Criticism 58*, no. 2, Improvisation in the Arts (Spring 2000), 157.

Structure is always a part of improvisation. Structure is necessary in worship for improvisation to occur. When something is missing, when someone doesn't show up to do their work, we must either improvise or stop. Without improvisation, we could just leave parts of the liturgy behind, instead of remembering the larger purposes of our gathering.

Improvisation is physical, either in its creation, performance, or reception. Improvisation is relational; it is a way of making something new between two or more people. The relational quality of improvisation means that it will transform worship on the basis of who shows up. Improvisation in worship is not done for the sake of novelty. Improvisation contrasts with novelty in as far as it seeks immediacy and working with what is currently available to both make something new and to honor the received tradition. But at its best it does much more. At its best, improvisation attends to a deep resonance that pervades creativity. It will just work. It will be right. And improvisation will present to the worshippers a new world that is still related to the old world of the tradition. Improvisation accepts the world that is with all of its surprises, limitations, and promises.

About ten years ago I was standing at the altar preparing myself to chant the Eucharistic prayer. A seven-year-old girl named Trinity came up to me and asked: "Can I help you today?" I was holding the notebook that contained the script for the service, so I handed that to her. I thought that would be enough work for Trinity, but it wasn't. I began the chant—the people were gathered close around the altar, and Trinity stood right beside me. As I chanted she drew closer and closer to me, until she was standing between the altar and me. I glanced down at her and saw that she had set down the notebook and was holding her hands up, just like I was, in the traditional attitude of prayer we call *orans*.

I concluded the prayer, and as we broke the bread, Trinity asked me, "Can I help you with the bread?" Who gets to serve communion is one of those things that some Episcopalians get hung up on. In some churches, people have to be trained in Eucharistic Ministry before they receive a license to serve the bread and wine. But in that moment at the altar all I could think to say was "yes." I gave her a paten of bread to lift up. Then the two of us gave communion to the gathered assembly, me steering Trinity through the standing crowd and offering chunks of bread, whispering in her ear the names of those she was communicating. Solemnly she would reach up and place bread in hungry hands saying, "Betsy, the Body of Christ."

During the coffee hour, which followed the service, I was talking to some visitors. Other people, including Trinity, were straightening up the seats, picking up used leaflets and music books. She came to me and asked, "Will you help me pick up the music books from the chairs?" The division of labor between children and clergy was completely opaque to Trinity. She and I were the people who served communion; why shouldn't I help clean up the church? I have experienced many miracles at the altar. But I have never stood at the altar and encountered God so directly in a moment of improvisation. Nor have I quite so strongly experienced the need to offer the gifts of God completely freely. The pure audacity of Trinity's request—the same sort of audacious request that God always makes of us—caught me up short and reminded me that God comes to us in every experience, ready or not.

❧

Sermon sharing—the people's responses to the preacher's sermon—is somewhere between a Quaker meeting and an AA group. Like those two spiritual traditions, sermon sharing at St. Gregory's is a time for people to testify to the presence of God, Light, Spirit, Higher Power in their lives. During our weekly staff meetings, we talk about the liturgy for about half an hour including what happened in sermon sharing. Over the years, we've learned that the more the preacher is grounded in his or her own experience, the more the preacher talks about what's really happening in his or her life, the richer the sermon sharing tends to be. We strive to preach in a way that makes theology out of narrative, not the other way around. The preacher is a story-teller as much as anything, but the story cannot be a decorative addition to a sermon; the story is the essence of the sermon.

The moment I always expect something to happen is after I've finished preaching and I ask the congregation to share their own experiences. There is a minute of silence at the end of the sermon; its beginning is indicated by ringing deeply pitched Japanese temple bells, its ending by high-pitched Tibetan tingsha cymbals. On days when I am less centered in myself, that minute of silence is when I think, "What have I done?! I've just preached a perfectly acceptable sermon, and now I have to let everyone else have a turn? What am I—crazy?" But on days when I am centered in the Spirit, I wonder what more God has to say to us. The Word is spoken by newcomers and old timers, by children and elders, and everyone in between. Of course, there are people who always want to talk, either out of anxiety that no one else is talking, or perhaps because no one listens to them anywhere else in their lives. The preacher has to call on people to share, which is always an exercise in holding the space and the assem-bly's energy. I seldom have to interrupt people in sermon sharing and redirect them to their experience, but when I have to I do.

Sermon sharing is risky. It invites both the best and the worst qualities of group dynamics. There are days when I think, "Maybe we'll just skip that part," but that's usually a sign of my anxiety, unaddressed by humility and love. Sermon sharing is among the most valued parts of our liturgy. We continue the practice because our community is committed to listening for God's revelation in the everyday occurrence of beauty, our gath-ering for worship, and striving for justice. We want to see more of what God is doing in the world. People need a place to share stories, including their experiences of how God is at work in their lives. I see the power of transformation when people share their own experiences after the sermon. In fact, these are some of the ways that sustain my life in God. The liturgy is always a reminder that God is breaking into our lives right now, making everything new.

God has an indiscriminate desire for us. As Ginny put it during sermon sharing one Sunday, "Jesus is sneaky! He just sort of sneaks up on you." When Jesus sneaks up on us, it isn't to scare us: Jesus sneaks up on us because of his desire for us. Our desire, as unclear as it can sometimes become, is the part of us that most closely resembles God. Ginny's insight about Jesus sneaking up on her isn't just about being surprised by love in her life; it is all about Jesus's desire to surprise everyone with the outrageous love of God. God's love puts a question mark over everything that we think we know about the world and the way it works to commoditize us. We listen to both individual and corporate experiences for God speaking. This is a theology that we get from the namesake of our congregation. Gregory of Nyssa taught that God's actions are what make God known, not just ideas about God. He wrote, "God becomes visible only in his operations, and only when He is contemplated in the things that are external to Him."[9] Just as people know God through his acting in creation, so we come to know God by hearing each other's stories of God's action in their lives.

Worship prepares people to go into the world with eyes open to seeing God at work. When we gather for worship, we are bathed in sacred story and action that is transformative. We are empowered to look at the world through the lens of God's love for all beings. When we forget to do this, it results in an experience of worship that is privatized, not communal. Personal piety doesn't have to be excluded from worship, but piety always depends on the larger work of looking at the world with love and acting out of that love. If worship is only mysterious and beautiful, it deforms people and makes them little

---

9   Paulos Mar Gregorios, *Cosmic Man: The Divine Presence; The Theology of St. Gregory of Nyssa [Ca. 330 to Ca. 395 A.D.]* (New York: Paragon House, 1998), 70.

more than consumers of the rites without any expectation that they will make something out of the experience.

I have discovered that worship has real power to change people's lives. And sometimes that's the problem: sometimes people prefer to be left alone, to live autonomously and not have to look at the messiness of another person's experience. It's like the man in another church I worked for. When it came time to exchange the peace, he would always kneel down and press his head against the pew in front of him. The idea of having to touch another body, of having his private experience interrupted by the messiness of another life, was just unbearable. But if we don't leave space for people to touch us, if we are satisfied with worship that does little more than scratch the surface of people's lives, I think we have to ask if worship is worth the effort. If isolation and superficiality is all that we have to bring, maybe worship is just another power that is seeking to deform people rather than build them up. And, of course, this is a very risky proposition. But the risks really are worth it. Without taking risks in worship, we may find that all of our work is worthless.

Jesus's promise is that whenever two or three are gathered together in his name he will be in our midst. His presence isn't just for our comfort; it is to drive us to action, looking for God at work in the world. If worship can free people to make meaning of their experiences, it can move them toward action in the world. In the same way that transformation takes place along the axis of head, heart, and body, worship influences people along an axis of meaning making and action. It isn't enough to have good thoughts about people or a theoretical approach to loving our enemies. Real action, rooted and growing out of real insights made in worship, has to happen if people are going to live fully as God's own.

All of these energies have to be in balance if worship is going to fulfill its transformative potential. If worship only provides an opportunity for personal reflection, then it very easily devolves into private time with God. If worship only pays attention to justice in the world, then it becomes a religiously tinged social work. Cassie, a parishioner who drives an hour and half with her partner every Sunday to be with us, comes because what she receives in worship reminds her that God is at work in the world just as surely as God is present in worship. Not long after joining the church she told me, "We came to St. Gregory's because you actually talk about God. The church we went to before spent all of their time talking about drone strikes in Pakistan." When the deep desire for an experience of community, bound in God's Spirit, is joined with a longing to see the world transformed by the loving power of God, then worship finds its truest purpose. From this perspective, neither personal spiritual experience nor social justice is sacrificed. Instead, a new optic is opened through which to see the world as God sees it. We are called to love others in real terms that are energized by the ever flowing of God's love through us and into the world.

⚒

The first time I baptized someone, it was in a delivery room at St. Luke's Hospital in Houston. I was in the last weeks of my clinical chaplaincy internship, a few short weeks after my ordination to the diaconate. I was on call that night, sleeping at the hospital. We only got calls in the middle of the night for very serious problems. The call I received from the nurse's station in labor and delivery was to attend to a woman who had delivered an anencephalic fetus. The nurse said, "You need to come up here and baptize this baby." He was nowhere near full term. And I didn't really understand what I was doing. You baptize living people, not dead fetuses. At least that's what I thought. But I knew that there was some pastoral necessity for this family, some need for closure.

I entered the patient's room. The nurse took charge of me, "Here," she said handing me a bottle of saline solution, "Use this." The body was wrapped in a blanket, and a tiny cap was on his misshaped head. The nurse handed me the bundle, and I poured water on his head, "I baptize you in the Name of the Father and the Son and the Holy Spirit." It was so difficult for me to look into his face. I handed him to his father who stood at his wife's bedside, and he simply dissolved in tears. When Jesus came to be baptized by John in the Jordan, John at first refused. Jesus's reply came to me as I witnessed this father's baptism in tears: "It is fitting that we should, in this way, do all that uprightness demands."

So many of my colleagues who have served in chaplaincies have told me similar experiences. Baptizing those for whom there is no clear theological category. But being obedient to the call of nurses—those first pastors to the sick—and doing what righteousness demands creates a new way of seeing God at work. It isn't about being right. It isn't about maintaining a clear theological line. It isn't about understanding what we are doing. Whenever we baptize, it is about being obedient to the love of God and the intention of God that nothing ever is lost, that everything is seen by God's love, and that everyone is transformed in that love. When we baptize, it is a way of saying that God's life will always take the place of our death.

The whole point of the Christian life is not to "patch up" a broken and distorted appreciation of the self, the world, and the other; it is to be remade, to be raised from the dead, to be unbound and placed in the midst of the living. The sacraments open us to a new appreciation of the gift of God's grace and the power of God's healing. But such dramatic transformation can only take place if we approach worship, the liturgy, and the sacraments as alive and available to those who come to worship. Esoteric rituals are not enough to bring transformation to people's lives. We can't "perform" the liturgy in a vacuum as if people's longings don't matter. If the liturgy is structured in such a way that it keeps worshippers from bringing their full, lived experience to the assembly, then it is just so much play-acting.

Something always dies when we take theological risks in worship. But it isn't the life that God loves; it is our certainty about how things should operate in this world. What dies is always the ideas and images of God that veer toward judgment. What dies is our need to be right. The good news is that we don't have to be right, because God is making righteousness happen in our lives right now and in every moment that we risk everything for the sake of transformation. That is when transformation happens in people's lives.

Last Easter I baptized Soren at the huge rock that is our font. It sits outside the church in a small courtyard behind the building, a few feet from the columbarium where we bury the ashes of our beloved dead. It had been more than a year since Soren and his family had been coming to St. Gregory's. He had grown more accustomed to the ways that we use worship to transform lives and was beginning to take a role in leadership at our early service. A natural musician, Soren would play the drum for our congregational dance. On the day of his baptism, I asked him the questions and renunciations that would mark the rest of his life: "Do you turn against evil . . . Do you accept Jesus Christ . . . Will you seek and serve . . . ?" Then we went out to the font. As he stood by the basin of the huge rock, I poured the cold water over his head: "I baptize you . . . ." With sweet smelling chrism, I marked him as Christ's own forever. When the baptism was completed, we went back into the church, and Soren got his drum, a huge, purple djembe, and beat out the rhythm for our final dance:

> This joyful Eastertide,
> away with care and sorrow!
> My Love, the Crucified,
> hath sprung to life this morrow.
> Had Christ, that once was slain,
> ne'er burst his three-day prison,
> our faith had been in vain;
> but now is Christ arisen,
> arisen, arisen, arisen.[10]

---

10 Words: George R. Woodward, 1894; Music: *Vruechten (This Joyful Eastertide)*, Dutch melody from David's Psalmen, Amsterdam, 1685, arr. Charles Wood, 1866–1926.

chapter

5

Singing: Having Music Within

This is the only church I've been in
where the job is truly handled by the
choir to lead the congregation in singing.
Every other church says that's the job,
and it's a lie, because their job is to sing
a beautiful anthem. And have everybody
sit in the pew with hands folded and say,
"Oh, the choir was so lovely today."
No, "The singing is so lovely"
is what it needs to be.

—*Randy B.*

I REMEMBER BEING ABOUT eight years old, showering in the downstairs bathroom of my family's home. The room was fully tiled, so it was a great place to sing. The warm water and the bright sound in that room got me singing. I don't remember what I was singing, but it was probably something I'd heard at church or on the radio. I sang out loud and clear, and, I thought, beautifully. But then I got out of the shower, dried off, wrapped the towel around me, and opened the bathroom door. There was my mother standing outside the bathroom smiling. It was clear to me that she had heard me singing. I didn't know that anyone could hear me singing in the shower. I was mortified, although I'm pretty certain her smile was about her love for me, and pleasure in hearing me sing. My face turned hot and red. I pretended that it wasn't me singing, but that lie didn't work. Being caught singing embarrassed me. As a result, my song was shut down. It wasn't because of another person's malice, but because I was ashamed to be heard singing. I didn't take up my song again for a very long time.

Eventually, when I found my voice, I studied voice. I sang in a couple of choirs in high school and college. I joined the choir of the Episcopal church where I was eventually confirmed. Today, people come up to me after church and say, "You have such a beautiful singing voice. You are so lucky!" I don't know if it's beautiful or not; it's loud, but that's not always the same thing. Whether or not it's beautiful, I love to sing. Singing fills me with a kind of pleasure that lifts me out of the ordinariness of life. But it wasn't always so. Early in my life, singing filled me with embarrassment, or worse it filled me with shame. I'm fortunate or blessed, or both, that I found a way to sing after not singing for so long.

For many people, the thought of singing starts a shame storm in them. Unless it's "Happy Birthday" or a sports chant or a drunken night of karaoke, most people would rather do anything other than sing in public. Having another person hear our voices in song can fill us with embarrassment or worse. If a schoolteacher or choir director tells a child that his or her voice isn't quite right, it can shut down their song forever. Many people who say, "I just can't sing," mean, "I just can't stand the thought of someone else hearing my song." As a society, we are leaving our songs behind. Almost no one sings socially anymore. About the only place where there is an ongoing custom of communal singing is in congregations, and even that is becoming rare. It does not have to be this way. One of the gifts of congregations to the rest of society is the opportunity to sing with other people. Singing with a group gives us a new way to know people. Singing feeds our hunger for beauty. Singing gets people listening to other people. Singing changes people's relationships. Singing is a powerful influence in the process of transformation.

⚜

On All Saints Sunday, we process around the inside of the church building, singing our praises to God for the saints who have come before us. Unlike our other processions, we stay inside the building on All Saints Sunday so that we can look at the giant icon of dancing saints on the walls of the rotunda. The saints dance above us as we circle the room, remembering Li Tim-Oi and Paul Erdös, Andrei Rublev and Cesar Chavez. At three points in the procession, we stop at stations to offer prayers. At the Day of the Dead shrine, we pray for our beloved dead. At the font, we pray for the host of martyrs. When we come to the icon of Mary, which hangs by the door to the kitchen, we pray in communion with the Mother of Jesus. I chant a verse that I stole from an Anglo-Catholic Socialist webpage: "Blessed be the Great Mother of God, dragging down tyrants. Blessed be Mary of Galilee, exalting the humble." I swing the thurible of incense and beseech God to hear us: "Grant us who honor the exaltation of her lowliness to follow the example of her devotion to your will." In our song and our walking, we bind our hearts to those who dwell in inaccessible light around the heavenly throne. That thin veil that divides the living from the dead grows thinner as we sing, remembering all that awaits us. It is as if our little procession is a part of the whole Communion of Saints, moving ever closer to God. And there at the head of our procession is Mary urging on our song.

Luke's gospel is full of song. Mary arrives, unannounced and pregnant, at the home of her cousin Elizabeth and the scene ends in song: "My soul magnifies the Lord." In the next scene, Elizabeth's husband, Zechariah, takes the stage to praise God's strong, stick-by-you love to the people at the birth of their son, John: "Blessed be the Lord God of Israel, looking favorably on us and redeeming us." After Jesus is born, the angels tear heaven open and sing their heads off about the glory of God that is crashing into our world: "Glory to God in the highest heaven, and on earth peace among those whom he favors!" And then old Simeon will creak through his song of mercy spreading from the light of the baby Jesus: "My eyes have seen your salvation." When people come to the limits of their lives, they sing. People sing in these liminal spaces because singing is the only thing that makes sense when you're faced with a mystery.

Mary's song is particularly powerful in the face of the mystery that she bears in her body. She sings it as if the good news she bears is already accomplished: "You cast down the mighty from their thrones and lifted up the lowly." She recognizes something about God that we still have trouble getting: God is siding with all of the beaten and excluded people that have dared to sing in the face of suffering and subjugation. Ever since there have been people who are denied their essential dignity, God has been right there, right next to them, preparing a way out of all that darkness. God has always been like this, and the ones like Mary, the ones who see that truth plainly, finally have all of the world's power; that is worth singing.

The domination culture under which we struggle encourages another song; a kind of light rock of this present age that demands nothing from us but sentimental nostalgia or projected rage. That song comes in so many different versions, from national anthems to mayonnaise commercials, but it will always render us less than God's beloved. Or we may listen to those mopey, morose ballads that my friend Amy used to describe as "music to open a vein to." And yet we claim the right that God gives us to pay attention to the Good News, and sing in the face of the bad news. Singing lifts us out of the world where the weak are dominated by the powerful, and the shame of the ashamed is increased. Singing helps us to see the world the way that God sees it: always filled with the potential for transformation and beauty.

When we take up Mary's counter-cultural song, we can actually sing out our lives not for what they are now, but for what God promises: a life full of courage, freedom, and love that imitates the same stick-by-you-ness that is the very definition of God's love. The God whom Mary sings is the God who delights in what is small and insignificant in the estimation of all the big deals and power brokers in the world. It is God's delight to take the most insignificant people imaginable and give them the power to do extraordinary and unimaginable things. That is God's promise. The voices that gather on a Sunday morning may seem like a small thing in the face of the worries of this present darkness. But it has always been from such small things that greater light spreads across the world.

※

Our Good Friday liturgy is one of the most beautiful, heart-breaking experiences of worship I've ever experienced. We sing deeply sad hymns, hear readings from Scripture, offer prayers for the whole world, join in chanting the story of Jesus's passion and death, lay flowers around an icon of Jesus's dead body and, when we have nothing else to give in prayer but our bodies, we solemnly prostrate ourselves on the floor around the altar.

I was sitting next to my colleague Sylvia during our Good

Friday service. As we sang, I could hear her voice, pure and high. After singing the first stanza of the hymns in unison, we broke into parts. I sang the lower, bass line while Sylvia stayed on the melody. Behind me, another woman's voice sang in a velvety alto, in front of me Sanford, our music director, sang in his impeccable tenor. The music was more than a single person could produce, more than an organ or guitar could create. From each of our bodies, we were making music that relied on every other body in the room. We sang John Bell's remarkable hymn:

> *Before the World Began, one word was there; grounded in*
> *God he was, rooted in care; by him all things were made,*
> *in him was love displayed, through him God spoke and*
> *said, "I am for you."*[11]

In the same way that God has always been for us, we are there singing for each other: "I am there for you, Sylvia. I am there for you, Sanford. I am for you." Our voices re-echo the depth of God's love for each one. It is not for me alone, not for my single voice that God was willing to be humiliated and die; it is for all of us. Our life together depends, not on my perfection, but on our mutual reliance on the God who loves each of us unendingly:

> *Life found in him its source, death found its end; light*
> *found in him its course, darkness its friend; for neither*
> *death nor doubt nor darkness can put out the glow of God,*
> *the shout, "I am for you."*

As our voices continued to interweave, I began to weep. All of the suffering, dying ones who fill my heart came to mind. Then I was aware that the suffering, dying ones are not only those who are known to me. Those unknown to me suffer the same pain, die in the same pitiful way. My single voice, my

11 John Bell, *Before the World Began*, Wild Goose Resource Group, Iona Community, admin. GIA, 1995.

particular experience of death, is not sufficient to encompass all that we mean when we come to worship on Good Friday. It is a communal lament, a public place for tears and weeping. Not only do we mourn for what we know, but we also mourn for strangers:

> *The word was in the world which from him came; unrecognized he was, unknown by name; one with all humankind, with the unloved aligned, convincing sight and mind: "I am for you."*

When we sing together, we pray twice. First, our minds are filled with images and ideas, but then our hearts are filled with the deepest longing, the most profound sense of beauty. When we sing together, we learn to hear not only how the other person's voice sounds, we learn something about who the other person truly is. We learn to extend ourselves not only into what we know but also into the unknown other, the stranger, all those for whom Christ Jesus lived and died and rose again.

Singing transforms everything, particularly in congregations. But it only has this power if congregational leaders give people the freedom to sing. The problem is that most congregations seem to go out of their way to stop people from singing. Just notice what happens when you walk in on a Sunday morning. Before people even have the opportunity to open their mouths, an organ begins playing the prelude. Or maybe the praise band cranks up, getting the congregation warmed up for the pastor's message. These can be beautiful pieces of music, but they are overwhelming to our voices. No human voice can ever hope to compete with a pipe organ or an amped-up praise band. Try singing along with the organ or the band; all you hear is the clamor of the instruments and your own still, small voice distantly in your head. Not only that, you can hardly hear the other voices in the room. Organists and praise bands just can't help it. When a professional begins playing music in church, it can invite the same shame and dread felt by someone caught singing, unaware: my voice isn't enough.

One way around this is to sing *a cappella*. St. Gregory's has always done this: singing without musical accompaniment, in four-part harmony. We sing without instruments, which allows us to listen carefully and pay attention to what we hear around and within us. Anything that we can sing, we do sing. We sing hymns. We chant the psalms. We sing the Lord's Prayer. All of the prayers at the altar are sung. Sometimes we sing the gospel reading. Alleluias ring out throughout the service during every season of the Church year.

One of the tricks that we employ in worship is to have the choir sit among the people. Unlike other churches where the choir sits removed from the people in their own little space, at St. Gregory's you are likely to be sitting right next to or in front of a gifted singer. When we begin to sing in harmony, the music is happening right around you. Which means that if you want to sing a vocal line other than the melody, you may hear it near you. If you listen, you may be able to sing in a way that you never knew you could before. Singing like this opens us up to transformation.

�֍

Sometimes when we sing together in worship, we screw things up. Either the notes are wrong, or the rhythm is off, or someone gets choked up, or we just sing the wrong thing altogether. I was standing at the altar, singing the Eucharistic Prayer in what I thought was a beautifully improvised chant tone. At one point, I either went too high or forgot to pause for a breath. Whatever happened, my brain cried out—BREATHE NOW—and I attempted to take a breath, only to swallow what little saliva was in my mouth. I began to cough and sputter, and because I didn't want the congregation to think that I was about to pass out, I said, "I'm okay—I just swallowed my spit!" Which was about the most undignified thing I think I've ever said in church.

Another time, I was standing up in front of the congregation, just beginning the Palm Sunday service, chanting the opening greeting, "Blessed is the king who comes in the name of the Lord." But someone had forgotten to announce the page number of the sung response. A few people kind of mumble-chanted a response, "And also . . . peace on earth . . . with you . . . glory in the . . . ." It was a train wreck.

At that point in the service, it would have been easy for me to pretend that I wasn't listening and just plow through with the next bit of chant. That might have been a more dignified approach, certainly more dignified than my experience choking at the altar. But that kind of polite, dignified ignorance didn't seem right that morning. Ignoring what is happening in people's lives is hardly ever the loving thing to do. Instead, I just stopped the liturgy and said, "Let's try that again." We got people on the correct page and started all over.

Loving people because of, not despite their imperfections, is vital. Loving our imperfections when we sing, coming back around to the place where we made a mistake and correcting it, tells people that listening matters and imperfection is not the worst thing possible. Listening and responding with love creates transformative moments in people's lives.

The way that we listen to each other creates the world in which we become whole. We are called to love each other before anything else. Before justice, or fairness, or parity, or purity, there must be love. Love is, before anything else, a choice about the other rather than a feeling about the other. I choose to love. If I choose to love you, then that love will be the thing that creates the world. If I am going to love you, then I need to listen to your voice; I have to attend to what you are saying. Becoming whole requires a habit of listening. The word that resides in our hearts and on our lips is a presence that is given freely to us. But if we don't listen to that word, then it has little power in our lives. Like any discipline, listening requires practice and consistency. And when we fail to hear, it requires us to return and start over. Singing together is one of the most powerful ways that we have to learn how to listen to each other.

When we sing together, the whole congregation agrees to be in a relationship of mutual obedience with each other. The word *obedience* is often confused with other words, like submission. But obedience is different. The word comes from the Latin root oboedire that means "to listen to." When we are obedient to each other, we are listening to each other. If we want to make music together, then we have to listen to what the other is singing. This discipline creates a space where we can also be obedient to God, listening to what God is saying to us individually and corporately. Singing together creates an opportunity for each one of us in the assembly to let the other person's voice have as much importance as our own. Listening to the singing of the whole community creates beauty, and it also tunes us to hear the rich, many-voiced voice of God.

St. Gregory's founders emphasized the power of music as perhaps the most significant tool for transformation. People come to St. Gregory's because each person's voice matters in making the community's song. Margaret was raised in the Episcopal Church but stopped attending in her early adulthood. When she was ready to come back to church, she came to St. Gregory's. She says, "I guess over the years I have a really strong sense of community here, and I didn't so much before." Margaret has found that she loves to sing; she finds this a transformative experience. She told me, "I have gradually learned to stay relatively on pitch and to sing lustily. And that's a heart expander, to do that." For Margaret, singing is not just beautiful; it opens a new appreciation of herself and the community.

✼

Our music director, Sanford Dole, is currently the longest serving member on our staff. He came to work at St. Gregory's before we moved into our building in 1995. Sanford has seen many changes over the years, and is the bridge between the period when the founders of the church were the rectors and when I became rector in 2008. Every Thursday night he gathers our gifted, volunteer choir for rehearsal. Some are trained musicians, some don't really read music very well; Sanford works with them all. They practice the music for the coming Sunday and for future concerts, always breaking to share cake and tea. Over the years choir members have moved away, their places taken by new singers who come to St. Gregory's. If there is a common thread that ties the choir together, it is Sanford and his joy in making music. More than once a member of the choir has said to me, "Sanford loves the music out of us."

Sanford also loves the music out of the congregation. At the beginning of every service he tells people, "Everything that you need to fully participate is in your music books. Keep those with you at all times and we will make a beautiful liturgy together." He leads enthusiastically, never telling us that what we're about to do is hard or impossible; and he never says ". . . if you're comfortable." Telling people to participate if they're comfortable always implies that what we're asking is really going to be uncomfortable.

.People join congregations for different reasons. Some come because it is a habit, like smoking or going to the gym. Some come because it is a point of human contact removed from the dehumanizing exchange of the workplace. Some come because it is the place where, for just a moment every week, what makes us real is freely given to everyone without exception. We all come to the church for different reasons. But we must, if we're honest, come because we need each other's support to grow in love and service. Like the members of our choir, people come to church because they want to have something "loved out of them," and in turn to love others.

In order to see Christ in our midst, we need each other. This is the claim that Jesus makes on the wild mix of people that he calls his church. No matter what we do, or what we believe, or how we feel about each other when we come together, Jesus is present in our midst. Not like a fourth player required for a game of bridge. Not as a third or fourth to our two or three. Jesus is present in our midst, among us in our relationships. And I take this to mean that whether we are fighting with each other, or sniping behind each other's backs, or weeping over each other's losses, or celebrating the glories that creep from time to time into our lives—in every place in our life together, Jesus is present. Whenever Jesus is present, transformation is abundantly available. This includes the times when we come together in song.

I was talking to Jessica about the ways that I saw transformation happening in people's lives, including those times when we sing together. She smiled when she reminded me that she came to St. Gregory's because she decided that she wanted to become an opera singer. The only problem was that she didn't know how to sing. Jessica had been a banker earlier in her life, at a time when that profession didn't particularly welcome women. Jessica had to fight every day to earn the respect that men were regularly given in the banking world. Being a trail-blazer in so many other ways, she believed that she could find a way to make her dream happen. She began to look at places where she might learn how to sing.

A friend suggested that if Jessica wanted to learn how to sing, she ought to sing in church. She started visiting and found that the community welcomed her voice. She's been singing for over eighteen years, although she has left behind her dream of becoming an opera singer. Instead, Jessica has developed a deep, mystical appreciation for her voice and her song. She says, "My voice today is so different than when I started singing, and the way I am in the world is so different." Instead of fighting her way through life, Jessica uses the power that she receives in singing to engage the world in new ways. She listens more carefully to what others have to say; she listens because her voice depends on the voices of others. She told me, "I listen a lot better in terms of other people. I think that singing has given me an intentional focus . . . holding a container for other people's growth and other people's pain, actually." Singing with other people has changed Jessica. Not only has it given her a way of experiencing beauty, it has given her a new way in which to engage with other people. Jessica's song has changed her life.

�֍

I was sitting in a monastic chapel with a group of other clergy, singing our way through a celebration of the Eucharist. The room was beautiful: an impossibly high ceiling and light-colored, carved stone. The acoustics were remarkable for congregational singing: I could hear my voice as well as the voices of my colleagues, blending in a single song of praise. But then I noticed that a woman sitting near me had forgotten that there were other voices in the room. She began to sing louder and louder, her eyes closed in a blissed-out state. Instead of a single chorus of voices singing together, we became a collection of individuals making our individual songs. Maybe this is a particular problem for clergy: we get so used to feeling like our leadership is the make-or-break reality in worship that if we don't sing loudly, then nobody else will either. It's like trying to push a rope: the harder you push the sound out, the more obnoxious you become.

We get so used to hearing our own voice as the only reference for what is real, which is just another way that we opt out of relationships. If you are the only self that you need to attend to, then you cannot have real relationships with anyone—including God. That's when it's easy to lose a sense of the image of God in the other person. But it is always God's pleasure to be found in the song of each one we encounter. Singing affects the way that people listen. The effect of singing creates a generous space for loving other people. Singing together changes our perception of others; it creates a space where we become more conscious of others, ready to hear other people's voices. Singing

115

together is an invitation to mindfulness, to listening not only in the moment, but also in the lives we live outside of worship. Singing together prepares us to listen to the voices of strangers, to the voices of people who are unlike us.

Singing together is always about living in relationship. Choosing to trust ourselves in relationship with others is always an invitation to transformation; we simply can't be in relationships without them making us new. Most of the time, this is a good thing. The gospel message is about changing relationships. Change is the good news—and it's also the really hard news. It's hard because it means that, if we want to experience transformation in our lives, we have to look out from our own experience and find our meaning in the lives of others. We have to step out of the center and move to the perimeter so that we can see all of the others who bear God's image. In the same way, when we're singing with other people, we have to hold the other person's voice with the same regard as we hold our own. It isn't enough just to sing loudly; we have to sing in a way that makes it possible to hear everything else that's going on in the room. This is hard because you can worry so much about how your voice sounds that you forget to listen to other people's voices. Then you're just making noise, maybe beautiful noise, but you are not making music with other people.

Brian works in human resources for a major corporation in San Francisco. His work can be challenging and stressful. He came to St. Gregory's when he began dating his husband. I asked Brian what difference beauty at St. Gregory's made to him. He talked about singing in worship, ". . . just knowing that we're all different individuals, but that we're sitting there and we're singing together. If I know that I'll have to have a difficult conversation within the next week, I remember how we harmonize together." Brian finds that singing with other people changes his perception of others, including those in his office. Like Jessica, he has discovered that singing with others opens a space to become aware of other people's experiences.

This awareness creates the capacity for him to empathize with others, listening to their perspective as well as attending to his own. Singing together is a skill that influences every part of our lives; it binds us in relationship with each other.

⌘

Tom was a member of St. Gregory's who died a few years ago. Tom was an entirely original person. Every Sunday he came to church he wore a kilt. He had long, flowing gray hair that he would occasionally wear in a neat bun on top of his head. From time to time, Tom would wear his beloved mother's brooches and earrings. Tom became sick just before Christmas and died the following spring. Because he couldn't care for himself, he entered hospice in a cognitive care facility. It was the kind of place that could be chaotic: many times when I visited, an elderly woman would wander into Tom's room, forgetting where her room was. It was noisy and smelled heavily of old bodies and bad food. It was precisely the kind of place that people tend to avoid: too much unpleasantness, too much pain. But St. Gregory's members continued to visit Tom in the many months that he was dying. Very often, when we visited, we would sing together.

Singing at people's sick beds began as a natural extension of praying with those who are sick and near death. Because so much of our worship is singing, it's only natural that those who go to pray and anoint the sick and dying also sing. Whenever we gather in song around the sick and dying, people's lives are transformed. Mark is a member of St. Gregory's who works as a hospital chaplain. He shared his experience of singing at another member's deathbed: "We had heard enough stuff and had sung enough things that we could sing around the bedside of this dying man. So having that music not only in *my* head but in *our* heads gave us a shared identity" (emphasis mine). Singing at a deathbed is about creating beauty; it is also about the relationships that we hold in common and that bind us together. Singing binds us to those who are suffering; it binds us to each other.

Singing together is critical. It shapes the ways in which we imagine ourselves, our relationships, and our ability to minister to other people. Music is not only the work of the choir or of those who are particularly adept at singing; it is something that anyone can do in the regular course of pastoral ministry. Randy relates a similar experience of singing at the deathbed of a parishioner, "People could hear us down the hall, and they sort of gathered around outside to be a part of making that a bigger experience by listening." Prayer and singing at the deathbed of beloved friends expand transformation to the lives of strangers and casual witnesses; it manifests the love of God to the world.

I understand love to be a kind of spiritual discipline. When I was falling in love with the man who is now my husband, I thought at first that it would be just the most natural thing in the world, sort of like breathing or drinking water when you're thirsty. But it was more like learning to ride a bicycle: if you think about it too much you can't do it, but once you have that motion in your muscles you never forget how to do it. It isn't true to say that I fell in love, it was more like I learned how to love—and once I learned it, I couldn't forget it. It took effort, and it took patience. I had to let go of my idealized notion of what love was supposed to be and just love. This is what it's like to share love in relationship in congregations.

People come to church to make relationships with each other based on a choice to love. This doesn't mean that we necessarily like everyone else at church. Instead, it means that we do things together. We sing together, we work and pray together, we argue and disagree, we fix meals when someone falls ill or has a baby. We stay in these relationships all the way to the grave. Congregations are gathering places where people die. When people are in the process of dying, the community has the chance to come together and manifest the love that we choose to share in relationship. I have witnessed many ways that this kind of love is expressed at St. Gregory's, but none as powerfully real as when we sing together, surrounding the dying in love. This is love expressed as much by showing up as it is by showing affection. The love that so deeply presses into the wounded souls of those who witness their beloved dying is tough; it's the kind of love that doesn't go away when death comes close.

Singing together manifests the love of God in the world. To love in this way is to love despite the messes and losses of any one of our lives. To stand in this love is to look in the direction of those who are most like God: the weak, the vulnerable, the forgiving. That's why, when we gather at the deathbed or the sickbed of a friend, it is gathering in the presence of God. The weakness that rests in that sickbed is intimately known to God. When we gather at the bed of one of our beloved friends who has died or is dying, we hold the hope that the one we love is changing more and more into the Word, who was with God before the beginning. And this is because the Word has become so tightly woven into our lives that he will always be present in the great and small events of our lives, and of our deaths. These are the times that we, like the Word, are close to the Father's heart.

As Tom's life was slowly draining away, he was seldom alone. People from St. Gregory's gathered around him almost every week to sing. Even as he became more and more unresponsive, the love of this community for him was firmly present. When he died, he was not alone. I arrived at his bedside not long after. Although the nursing staff had covered his face with the bed sheet, his friends and I uncovered him. We were not afraid to see him as he was: really dead and still very much present. His long, flowing gray hair spread out behind his head like a halo. He looked like some Russian saint, his eyes vaguely fixed on a point beyond us that we could only hope to see. We stood strongly beside him even though he seemed very, very far away. We sang for him, and for ourselves: "Christ is risen from the dead, trampling down death by death and to those in the tomb bestowing life." Love like this is gospel love. Love like this transforms everything.

�֎

I came to be a baseball fan late in my life. I owe it all to the world's greatest baseball team, the San Francisco Giants. In 2010, one of the years that the Giants won the World Series, the final game coincided with another important date on the calendar: All Saints' Day. We don't have a liturgy on All Saints' Day at St. Gregory's. Like many congregations, we hold the celebration on the Sunday following, but All Saints' is one of my favorite liturgies of the Christian calendar. I sometimes go to another congregation to join their celebration of the myriad saints we hold in sacred memory. So, on November 1, 2010, I pulled on my Giants jersey and drove across town, parked the car, and stepped into the Church of the Advent.

The Advent has one of the most breathtakingly beautiful All Saints' High Masses imaginable. The congregation is, in some ways, quite different from St. Gregory's. They are the keepers of what Episcopalians call the "High Church" style of liturgy. Lots of damask vestments, lots and lots of incense, lots of processions, very formal, very beautiful liturgy. They have an exceptionally fine choir who sing the Mass for the congregation. It is at the Church of the Advent that I get to sing my very favorite All Saints' Day hymn: *Jerusalem the Golden*. I know that the hymn is a little over the top, a piece of Romantic-era music with cloyingly sweet lyrics. The harmonies tug the heart. It presses into an eschatology with which I have a bit of trouble. And I love it.

The Liturgy of the Mass, so colossally formal compared to the way we worship at St. Gregory's, began to unfold before me like a beautiful pop-up book. The vestments were sumptuous and all matched—something that just never happens at St. Gregory's. The singing was robust and heartfelt, if a bit drowned out by the organ. The sermon was delivered with a passion fueled by the gospel. The congregation members were polite, if not terribly outgoing at the Peace. Clouds of incense filled the room at all the right moments. Mystery filled every nook and cranny of the gorgeous room. And there was another celebration going on just down the street at the San Francisco Civic Center. A crowd of thousands gathered to watch the final game of the World Series on an array of big screens set up and down the plaza in front of City Hall. I will admit to being swept up in Giants fever, checking the score on my cell phone at the end of the sermon. Less than a quarter mile away, thousands of fans were watching the game. My people were in two locations at once: The Church of the Advent and the Civic Center.

Then it happened. The veil between the damask and incense and Giants' jerseys and baseball was torn apart. While the choir sang a beautiful *Sanctus* by Tomás Luis de Victoria, the Giants won the game and the Series. When it happened, I was piously bowing, listening to the music and praying with the assembly, but you could tell we had won the game by the muffled roar of the Civic Center crowd. Then there were car horns honking and firecrackers exploding. The sound inside and the sound outside merged and became one: a celebration of the sacred and the profane. As happens whenever the sacred and the profane are mixed, it raised the question of God's presence and plea- sure in creation. Listening to the music played by the organ and sung by the choir during the communion, hearing the crowds passing by the church on their way to bars and restaurants, all of the sounds generated a sense of joy and chaos and the unde- niable mixing of the clean and unclean which Jesus Christ came to bless. You could try and ignore either the sound of the Mass or the sound of the baseball fans, but blending them together struck me as a perfect way to celebrate the Feast of All Saints.

Just as singing does, transformation in life requires us to pay attention. Singing together requires a habit of listening, to each other and to the voice of God that is continually breathing through us. It is God who animates our song. This is the Word of God that is in our hearts and on our lips. Like any kind of discipline, singing out the Word of God requires practice and consistency. And when we forget our song, which we all do, it requires us to return to God and start over. Which is just the way that it is with anything that prospers us in life. God gives us his Word not to set us up for failure, but to abide with us forever. We get to sing out the Word with us wherever we go, and that song will transform us. And when we are transformed, becoming more fully ourselves, we can share the Word of God everywhere we go. Then you can do things that you don't expect and sing songs you're just beginning to hear.

After the celebration in Civic Center and the Church of the Advent that All Saints' Day, I met my husband Grant and we had dinner at a restaurant nearby. We toasted the Giants. We told stories of what we had seen and experienced that day. We drove home honking our horn and waving to the fans, still streaming through the streets. And the saints danced above us in their eternal and heavenly dance, following their leader who is the love of God made flesh. And I heard the sound of new life that God has given freely to all people. Listening, I heard the sound of joy.

Making: Permission to Create Beauty

*It's very nice to have permission
to create beauty. It is so pleasurable
and gratifying to have my work used.
You do art and it hangs on a wall,
maybe, if you're lucky in a gallery
somewhere, and people come and say,
"Hmmm, I don't know about that."
If it's an icon, they kiss it!*

—Betsy P.

I AM A MAKER as well as a priest. I paint and draw and assemble disparate objects into new things. I have a long relationship with making. I have explored a lot of the world, both inside my soul and in the world around me, by making stuff. Some of what I make is functional and straightforward; I'm one of those people who finds Ikea instructions to be pretty readable. I also make things that are complex and technical; I baked my first soufflé when I was ten years old. Like Betsy, I paint icons: abstract and honest depictions of the sacred other. In the theology of the Eastern Church, icons are said to share the fundamental reality, the *hypostasis*, of the one depicted. The essence of the one depicted is a part of the image. The reality of the saint and the image of the saint are mysteriously related. Icons are images of physicality as well as spirituality; they are beautiful as both. Icons are always images of human bodies: faces, torsos, hands, as well as groups of people depicted in nature or interiors.

Bodies have been depicted in Christian culture, as a way of prayer, since at least the third century. Bodies find their place in Christian devotion because the Word became flesh and dwelt among us within a culture that had a visual vocabulary of bodies. Portraits in late antiquity share many features in common with icons: large eyes, a calm expression that contains both energy and emotion, a flat plane that contains vivid color and energetic pattern. Images of human bodies have been used by Christians to see the holy in ways that are not ordinarily available. They have required the viewer to pay attention to the world in a particular direction: to see the holy not as abstraction or purity, but as physical. Images are used to imagine God and God's friends, not as thought or idea, but as compassionate, embodied others. In the eighth century, John of Damascus instructed us to greet icons with our lips as well as our hearts and eyes. That is why, in the devotional practice of the Eastern Church, icons are always kissed.

Painting icons is hugely physical, based in the earth's elemental stuff. Before I paint an icon, I prepare the elements that will become the sacred image. I grind pigments—some of which are poisons, some of which are jewels—with a glass muller on a ceramic pallet. I make tempera, the medium in which I mix the pigments, from egg yolks that I carefully extract from the yolk sack and mix with cheap white wine. When the whole image is complete, I anoint the finished icon with linseed oil, using my hands to smear the oil over the image, feeling the subtle grit of the paint on my palm. I use the stuff that makes me—water and minerals and fat and protein—to create images that try to give form to the formless, and I've done it with a certain measure of devotion. I seek to do what the writer of Colossians describes: to make visible the image of the invisible God. I have worked out my theology in paint and board, and I have sometimes worked it out with fear and trembling. I have battled my ego and my limitations. I have learned to rely more and more on the Spirit of God to guide my hand. So, when I talk about making beauty as a way of knowing God and being changed by God, I speak from deeply personal experience.

There is a particular icon, one that we use at St. Gregory's on Good Friday. It is an image that I painted, an icon called the *Epitaphios*, the burial icon of Jesus. The word *epitaphios* is a composite of two Greek words: *upon* and *grave*. The icon shows Jesus's dead body stretched out on a slab of rock. His eyes are closed; his face is peaceful. He is surrounded by weeping angels who hover above him, their hands covered in cloth as a sign of respect. Along the border are the gilded letters of a verse we sing on Good Friday: "The noble Joseph, when he had taken down your most pure body from the Tree, wrapped it in fine linen and anointed it with spices, and placed it in a new tomb." At the end of the Good Friday service, we carry this icon to the altar table in the middle of the huge rotunda and place it near the edge of the table, close enough so people can touch it. And then we sing psalms and walk in procession to the table with flowers in our hands and lay them on the table around the image of the dead body. People touch the image or lean down and kiss it. As the singing and procession continue, the flowers pile higher and higher until you can hardly see the icon anymore, only the cut flowers, which are also dying. So death and beauty and love and devotion are piled up. Symbol on symbol, image on image.

The masters of iconography teach that each step of painting an icon is a prayer, a way of attending to the beauty of God that you are trying to communicate in the icon. For the truly pious there is a prayer for each brushstroke. I am not that pious. But I do pray, sometimes haltingly and sometimes easily. Most of the time I pray for people I know and love, or know and don't love. But what is centering about painting an icon is the conversation with the figure being depicted. Sometimes I call on the figure to help me. I remind myself that God wants to be seen in the work.

I have learned that sitting in the presence of a dead body is an experience that can both unmake and remake you: it raises questions about your own mortality as well as the mortality of those you love. To paint an image of a dead body had a similar effect on me. When I was painting the image of Jesus stretched out dead on a rock slab, I was in a kind of intimate communion with his body. There have been other bodies stretched out before me, both the living and the dead, some for love and some for pity. But the dead body of Jesus was charged with a power that captivated me, and that I wanted to depict as well as I could. As I painted, I would enter into a devotional musing with Jesus. Sometimes, I would ask questions: *What was it like to be dead and then alive? Did it keep hurting until you were raised? Why did you still have the holes in your hands and feet and side, but not all the marks from the flogging?* My mind was centered on his body, and then on my body. Sometimes I would stop to take hold of my arm or leg, to feel my own muscles to make sure what I was painting looked like a real body. I painted, sometimes holding my breath to steady my hand, and then lifting the brush to inhale. It was like the breath of the Spirit entering my body. Every stroke of the brush was like a whispering of the Wisdom of God. Every mixing of pigment and tempera was a divine act of creation. Every prayer was a moment of recreation.

When I had finished the icon, before it was first used on a Good Friday, I blessed it during a Sunday Eucharist. Before we began the service, I set the icon in the middle of the altar table. Chalices and patens sat next to it. As happens every Sunday, we brought bread and wine to the table, blessed and broke it, then shared these gifts with the whole people of God, all of the friends and strangers who join us at the table Sunday after Sunday. At the end of the people's communion, I leaned over the icon, pressing my hands to it, and prayed God's blessing on the image. Making the sign of the cross three times, I pictured the icon serving as the center of people's devotion. Then I carried the icon through the assembly so that they could see it for the first time, gently touching their hands to it in blessing, leaning in to kiss the image. I had always intended to give the icon to St. Gregory's for our use on Good Friday. In blessing it, I was giving it away. The pleasure that I had in making the icon is now matched by my pleasure in seeing people use it for their prayer and devotion. My pleasure, through the icon, is given away to the people I love.

Our work in making beauty is analogous to the act of God in creation. The danger in this is confusing the created with the Uncreated; what I create will always be contingent on the glory of God that inspires all creation. The first icon I painted wasn't very good: the colors were muddy, and the lines were stiff. I was learning how to paint at a workshop. The teacher walked by as I was finishing the icon and said, "Don't worry. It'll look fine by candlelight." Even though my work wasn't perfectly executed, God's glory would still shine through. I gave that first icon away to a friend from the food pantry who lives alone in an apartment in the Tenderloin. She told me, "It's at the very center of my home altar, honey, right next to Ganesha."

✣

A few years ago I lost Jesus. I opened up the box that contains our Christmas crèche, and Jesus was nowhere to be found. I've loved crèches since the first one that my mom bought at Sears not far from my childhood home. I was fascinated by the tiny, plastic figures—each one precision cast and painted by hand, imported from Italy according to the label. I was the one who would carefully set the crèche up every Christmas. But being a crafty sort, it wasn't long before I made my first crèche. It was the 70s, and I made the figures as corn shuck dolls. This was during my back-to-nature phase of crafting. Later, the corn husks cracked and peeled apart; I made more elaborate figures from scraps of my sisters' prom dresses and broken bits of costume jewelry I swiped from my mother's bottom drawer—the drawer where the cheap jewelry was stored. When I left home, I left all the crèche figures at my parents' house.

When I was finally finished with school and found myself making Christmas in my own home, I knew that I had to have a Christmas crèche. I found some suitable figures carved out of olive wood in a shop and pieced together a crèche with them. By the time I moved from Texas to San Francisco, I had somehow added four additional magi to the crèche; they were all lost in the move. The first Christmas in our new home, I set up a crèche with new figures, a combination of gifts people had given me over the years and a particularly fabulous Pez dispenser. Most of the figures look like a cross between Indian and Ethiopian. This is the set from which I lost Jesus.

The Christmas I lost him, I left the manger bare. When people would ask where Jesus was, I'd say something about the body of Christ being in the whole people of God—or some kind of theological dodge. The next year I experimented with putting one of the animals in the manger—I recall a tiny bobble head turkey from Mexico—but it just didn't seem right. So last year I decided to replace the lost Jesus with one I made myself. I went to the bottom of the drawer of the workbench in the garage and got out the essential tools: a glue gun and the cheap costume jewelry that I'd pilfered years before from my mother's bottom drawer. I began to look for a suitable body for the Christ child. I went to the junk drawer in the kitchen; it contains everything that I can't find a suitable place for in the rest of the house. I began to look at my options.

I started with a champagne cork. Its bulbous end sort of looked like a head, and I imagined I could stick some little arms in it. But when I did, it ended up looking like a kind of wood-grained space alien. I tried whittling it down to a more anthropomorphic shape. But if you've ever tried to whittle cork, you know that it doesn't work so well. I abandoned the cork. I kept digging through the junk drawer, looking for a better base for baby Jesus. But there was nothing. Then I looked through the old plastic shopping bag that contained the pilfered costume jewelry from my mother. In it, I saw something that I recognized as a "worry doll"—something she brought back from a trip to Guatemala. The worry doll is a fabric doll that you're supposed to tell your troubles to, and then place under your pillow at night to assure a peaceful night's sleep.

The worry doll had a white muslin head with little eyes and a mouth stitched in black thread. It wore a little scrap of colorful Guatemalan fabric. The tiny hominid was perfect. I took a piece of silk I found in the junk drawer (don't ask me how it got there) and carefully swaddled the worry doll. I found a discarded button that was just the right size for a halo and hot-glued the whole thing into the manger. I assembled the crèche. It contained everything that Christmas needs: the mother and father, the two shepherds and three magi, the ox and ass and sheep, and the elephant and tiny armadillo and the even tinier turtle and the bobble head turkey and the Pez dispenser with a Santa head. At the center of the scene, I placed the beautiful swaddled Guatemalan baby glued to his manger. I hung a paper star from a bamboo skewer crammed into a crack at the top of the cabinet where we display the crèche. It was beautiful.

When God made himself in our human form, he came as the least likely form that we inhabit: a newborn baby. Born to peasant parents in the back of borrowed shed, God made herself at home in our human flesh and bones and spirit. And this was God's desire from all eternity. From before creation and forever it had been God's longing and hope to take on our fragile, sweet, human flesh. Even if we had done better than we seem to have—even if Adam and Eve had never strayed from the Garden of Eden into a life of suffering and death—even then God would have become fully human. God simply wanted to be with us as we are.

I tried to make a suitable baby Jesus for my crèche out of the stuff I found in the junk drawer and a bag of broken jewelry. God made herself the perfect figure to draw our love and adoration out of the precious stuff that is our human bodies. God made himself a baby, one who had to be cared for and nurtured and fed and protected. Unlike the baby that I made, God didn't need to be swaddled in silk and topped with a shiny, button halo. God came to be as simply and beautifully present with us as any infant. The crèche that I made told the story of the love and nearness of God to all of creation. The story says that God wouldn't be distant or strange. God wouldn't just be close to us in creation; God would be completely a part of it. We don't have to struggle to remake what is lost or repair what is broken. We don't have to achieve some idle dream of perfection or strive to do better next time. God comes to us in the simple, real things that make our lives.

The relationship between God as Creator and the artist as creator is based on the principle of making something out of nothing. When we make beauty, it is always informed by God's power of creation. When we make something, we begin with what is in front of us—even if that is an absence. We take what God gives us in creation, and we make something that hasn't been seen in exactly the same way before. In this sense, a work of art can be a part of the revelation of God. But this isn't something that only professional artists enjoy; everyone who engages in "making" participates in the same dynamic. When we work at making—art, vestments, poetry, music, food, software, anything really—we are imitating God's work in creation. We are co-creators with God, joining in God's dance of creation.

During our Sunday liturgy at St. Gregory's, we move from the seating area at one end of the building to the altar at the other end. We sing a hymn as we move, and we don't just ramble over from one side of the building to the other. Instead, we practice a kind of ritualized Conga Line: each person turns and faces the altar, placing their right hand on the shoulder of the person in front of them, and we walk together—three steps forward, one step back. I can still visualize the first time I visited St. Gregory's and walked with the assembly to the table. I can even remember the hymn that we sang as we moved together: the hymn *O Spirit of God, O Spirit of Life.* As we sang and moved, hands on shoulders and stepping together, I had that sense of forward motion that I know is God's invitation to transformation. "O Spirit of Life, O Spirit of God, in every need thou bringest aid, thou camest forth from God's great throne, from God, the Father and the Son; O Spirit of Life, O Spirit of God."[12]

God's Spirit is at work in every congregation's life. That is the reality that makes transformation possible. God's Spirit is always moving her people forward. But we never move alone; God's Spirit is at work as we come together in love to support and motivate one another to continue into the future that God dreams for us. My experience of moving to the table during the Sunday

12 The Episcopal Church, *Poems of Grace: Texts of The Hymnal 1982* (New York: Church Publishing, 1998), 417.

liturgy—that hand on the shoulder, three steps forward, one step back movement—continues with me because it makes tangibly real what God is always doing in our midst. We are transformed in relationship to each other. None of us takes on the work of making beauty in the church alone: we make church together.

Making beauty in the church is not simply functional; it isn't simply about getting someone to arrange the altar flowers or create a visually appealing bulletin or sing a gorgeous solo; it is always about building relationships. Over the years, St. Gregory's has found that creating beauty in the context of community encourages transformation in people's lives. Whenever people gather to make things together, our lives are changed.

In order for this to be transformative, everyone has to be invited into making beauty. Like every spiritual discipline, we learn and grow in our abilities as we make beauty at church. Working together gives us opportunities to share with each other the experience of creating beauty for the sake of the community, sharing stories, unfolding our shared history. Whether we are doing functional work like cleaning the kitchen or pulling weeds in the garden, or expressive work like painting icons or singing new music together, everyone is transformed by making. I know this through my own experience of making beauty with the members of St. Gregory's.

Holy Week is the high mark of our year. There are two seasons at St. Gregory's: Easter, and Easter Is Coming. The whole congregation is invited to come to the church and share the work of making beauty. During Holy Week 2015, I was at the church more hours than usual. The usual stress of liturgical preparation was compounded by the early date of Easter; it seemed like we had just put away the Christmas wreaths when it was suddenly Lent and everything that follows. All of the liturgies of Holy Week had been beautiful. I arrived at the church around 8:30 on Holy Saturday, ready to work through the morning with whoever showed up to work, getting ready for our main Easter liturgy, the Great Vigil.

We began moving the chairs and removing the black fabrics from the Good Friday liturgy. There were buckets of flowers sitting around the edge of the rotunda, ready to be arranged. Someone had gathered bales of jasmine vines from their garden to use. There were piles of silk saris to drape over and around the room. We had three hundred beeswax hand candles to prep and a hundred more beeswax candles to put into heavy, wrought iron chandeliers.

I was tired. As always happens when I'm tired, I forgot the most important piece of our Holy Week preparations: giving work away. I flew from one task to another, answered one question after another, found the tool someone else needed that I had set aside and forgotten. And it happened: I started to hate everyone. "Why can't you people just do this?" I asked myself, "What is wrong with you?!" The pity party started heating up. Sara gave me that look, the one that says, "I know what you mean—but ease up." I fumed, "Am I the only person here who cares about any of this?" As my millennial friend, Dani, later said, "You were like, #martyr."

I had to stop. I looked around the room and saw Laurie, a parishioner who has to drive two hours to get to St. Gregory's. She had just walked in the door and was looking for a job. The year before, she had been in charge of flowers, a job I was perilously close to assuming. "Laurie, I'm so glad you're here. Can you just take the lectern and make it beautiful?" I pointed to the buckets of flowers and piles of silk. "Of course, Paul. Don't worry. We've got this." Like a fever in the middle of the night, my sullen mood broke. "Of course, you've got this," I thought, "God built this church for all of you." I didn't have to carry this alone; I couldn't. I found myself enfolded in the strength and love of the community. "O Spirit of Life, O Spirit of God, make us to love thy sacred word; the holy flame of love impart, that charity may warm each heart; O Spirit of Life, O Spirit of God." Love won that day. Giving work away, trusting the community to carry me, believing that God wants to be known not only in me and my gifts, but in the giftedness of the whole congregation, saved me. Moving together as one Body, we found our work in our relationships. And Easter was glorious.

When people want to contribute to the beauty of the church with the work of their hands, congregational leaders are gatekeepers. Sometimes leaders trust that what the person brings will enrich our common life and easily say "yes" to the gift that is brought. Sometimes leaders are skeptical about the person and what they want to bring, and say "no." Congregational leaders have a responsibility to make these calls, but we have to keep our eye on the path ahead of us, and how the offerings that are brought from the work of people's hands lead us forward. In congregational life, this may be about making art or about making coffee or about making plans for what the community needs to learn together. People take a tremendous amount of pleasure in making things. Congregational leaders have to learn how to say "yes" more than we say "no." Saying "no" to people's pleasure in making limits those with the authority to make church. Every time that we limit the number of people with this authority, we diminish the whole community.

We recruit as many members of the congregation as we can for Holy Week and Easter preparations. There is a lot of work to share as we prepare our space for worship. Before the church is prepared for the Great Vigil of Easter, with its bright colors, shimmering silks, and piles of flowers, there is a week of liturgies. Each one has a distinct aesthetic quality that relies on changing one set of art objects for another. We hoist huge palm branches above the altar in the rotunda for Palm Sunday, covering tables and lectern and presider's chair in blood-red fabric. We transform the rotunda into a dining room for Maundy Thursday and hang lanterns in the front garden to which we process after the foot washing and solemnly pour the used water onto the ground. For Good Friday, the entire church is vested in black, using fabrics from many different sources, including sacred art from other religions. This is no small task. Well over fifty people are involved in preparing the space for Holy Week and Easter. Margaret reflects on her experience of working to create beauty: "The selection of the fabrics is just amazing to me. Learning to do things with flowers that I'm not particularly skilled or have any instinctive ability to do. But watching others and either mimicking or realizing but with a small change that reflects me." As she works with other, more experienced workers, Margaret acquires knowledge and skills that amaze and delight her.

I find the genius of Holy Week and Easter in the many ways that we work together to create something new. Even though the community of St. Gregory's has seen almost forty Easters together, every time we come to these days of wonder they are unique. There are things that stay the same. Good Friday wouldn't be the same without our solemn procession to the burial icon of Jesus, carrying both our love and flowers for his burial. Our Easter celebration would be diminished without that blast of light from the church following our nighttime vigil and procession. But the nuances and innovations and experiments we take on offer surprises and delight every year. This work comes from the heart and giftedness of our community, not from experts who have produced the full canon of church aesthetics.

✂

Touch is an essential part of the liturgy at St. Gregory's. Not only do we affectionately touch or kiss icons, we also reach out and lay our hands on those who come forward to receive a blessing. If an individual can't reach the person offering blessing, we tell them to touch someone who can. We reach out to touch the gospel book as the preacher carries it through the congregation after the sermon, and we move together to the altar resting a hand on the shoulder of the person in front of us. All of these touches add up. Not long ago, someone shared with me that the number of times we are asked to touch each other during the liturgy is around fourteen. Touch is one of the ways that we intentionally express the love of God in the midst of the liturgy. Touch is a metric that matters, and using our hands to touch is an expression of our great pleasure in making church.

About twenty-five years ago, after years of being stuck in my head, first as a student and then as a candidate for ordination, I decided to have a massage. I believed that touch would heal something inside me and help me to know my body as a place of God's wisdom. The first time I had a massage was at the hands of an aging hippie in Austin, Texas. His consulting room was in an office next to my brother's architecture firm. He worked with people on a mat on the floor, doing myofascial release. The technique has the therapist press into the soft tissue of your body until the fascia—the stuff that connects all your squishy innards—relaxes or releases. The key is sustained pressure over time. I found out that this kind of touch hurt. When it hurt, he encouraged me to make noise, and he would make noise with me. Like a birthing coach, he would moan with me and keen with me and join in making a kind of deep, guttural, animal howl. And whenever he felt something letting go in me, he would whisper encouraging words. It was a weird and sometimes scary way for me to try to connect with my body, but it began to heal me.

Throughout the Gospels, Jesus heals people by touching them. When he touches them, he makes something new between them; this is the essence of his power to heal. Just as God in creation brought form out what was unformed, so Jesus brings wholeness out of what is broken. The Gospels tell us that Jesus's touch is powerful. But the power is more than just taking away physical symptoms. His touch creates a relationship that is eternal. Jesus isn't like my old hippie massage therapist. He doesn't practice on you for an hour and then expect payment. When Jesus touches you, he stays with you. His touch makes people into members of his family.

In 2015, I was back at the Wild Goose Festival in North Carolina. It's a three-day gathering of a couple of thousand followers of Jesus who learn, pray, dance, make art, and are transformed. On the final day of the festival, there was an early morning healing service, held in the middle of the festival site, in a field surrounded by green trees. Although I hadn't planned on being there to pray with people, my friend Sara dragged me from the breakfast table and took me along. "They need you," she explained. We sang and prayed as a large group and then we who were tasked with laying our hands on people and anointing them went into the midst of the crowd and prayed. After several people had come to me for prayer, I saw a young man I had talked to the night before.

Nathan had come out as gay to a large group of people on the first day of the festival. For us in San Francisco, coming out stories are heard less and less frequently; so many of our young people come out early in their lives and with very little drama. But this man had been closeted his whole life, a lay minister in a large church, and he was afraid. The night before, we had talked about his feelings of shame and confusion and joy and delight. He worried about the response he would receive from his family and his congregation. I expected that he might come to me for healing prayer that morning, but he remained seated on the ground. When it seemed like no one else was going to come and ask me to pray, he caught my eye, and he beckoned me over. By the time I got to him, he had covered his face with his hands, sobbing. I knelt down before him on the dusty ground and did the only thing I could think to do: I wrapped him in my arms. There, in the midst of a crowd in the middle of a field on a muggy southern morning, I felt moved to act in a way that I did not understand, but knew was the right thing to do. The only thing that made any sense was to touch him.

After a while, holding Nathan in my arms, him sobbing and me soothing him, I began to speak. I can't remember what I said exactly, but it was a kind of healing prayer. I couldn't ignore a deep feeling within me, a feeling that brought words to speak. "You are so loved." "You are so courageous." "You are so frightened." The words were not like a formal prayer for healing; they were more of a mantra of what was happening in that small, holy moment. All I could do was to stay present, ignore the ache in my knees and my tear-drenched tee shirt, and allow myself to be moved by a power that was not from me. All I could do was hold Nathan in my arms and let the power of God work in him.

Jesus's compassion—his gut-deep feeling for the pain of the crowd—is a gift that he shares with each one of us. When you have that experience of feeling so deeply for another that you can't ignore it, it is the Spirit of Jesus at work in you. A long time ago Jesus looked over a dusty field by the Sea of Galilee, stopped his teaching, stood up and moved into the crowd laying his hands on the sick, making them whole. He was compassion incarnate that day, and the same compassion continues to flow in our lives today. When we feel the Spirit of Jesus stirring in our souls, we must act. Like Jesus, we may be on our way to rest, and the need of the world may get in our way. We may be on our way to work or study or play, and the need of the world may get in our way. Then we will have to change our plans and redirect our attention. Then we will begin to make the church alive in new ways. That's just the way it is when we choose to follow Jesus and be transformed by his touch.

I frequently talk about what we do at St. Gregory's as *churching*. When I was talking to Randy about my work of developing a theory of transformation in congregational life, I shared my hope that other congregations might find their own ways to make church more deeply. Randy paused and gave me a funny look, "You used what normally is a subject as a predicate: church. And I think that's what happens. I get to church. I get to be a part of a church, but also get to be the predicate church—we're all churching." Each person has a role to play in the process. Randy continued, "I'm just a small part of that, because everybody is making the music. Everybody is adding the prayers of the people. Everyone is finishing the sermon sharing. Everyone is decorating the church. We don't have a sexton. We all make coffee hour happen. We church." All of us have insight to gain as we try new tasks. When we do things that we don't know we can do, we find our competence and self-confidence growing. When we "church" together, we are transformed.

✄

I teach practical theology and congregational leadership to low-residency MDiv students as an adjunct instructor at the Church Divinity School of the Pacific. My students come with every imaginable kind of background: academics, law enforcement officers, retirees, social workers, and physicians. The common theme in their stories is the strong call of God to ordained ministry. All of the students have spent time churching, some as dedicated lay volunteers, some as employees of congregations. At the end of our two-week intensive, I assign the students case studies to which they have to respond, using the tools we learn in class. The case studies are all fictive: I have made up about ten different scenarios for them. The last one is about a turf conflict between competing needs in the congregation:

> *The St. Elizabeth's Altar Guild has always had the Christmas bazaar in the parish hall, the new rector plans an Advent program that needs the hall at the same time. What do you do?*

Everyone in the class got a knowing look when I read the final case study aloud. Turf is something that congregations just love to fight over. My most cynical statement about these turf battles is, "Congregations fight so hard internally because the stakes are so low." And yet, there is a sense in which these intra-congregational battles are such a trope that everyone can predict the battle lines that people will form. That's why St. Gregory's has never had an altar guild or any other such standing committee to make the church beautiful. We strive to prepare the church for worship on an ad hoc basis and encourage the whole congregation to participate under the leadership of anyone who feels the desire and vocation to lead. No one has to be an expert to do this; you just need a willingness to work lovingly with others. At St. Gregory's, making beauty is not just an isolated event that some few members take up in privacy; it is a public, relational, cooperative, messy, generative event in which everyone is invited to take a part. As Betsy says, "It's a very participatory congregation by design, but that really works . . . you don't have to fight your way through a committee as happens at many churches."

Congregations fail when they confine "makers" to a special class, or "beauty" to a specific canon, or "churching" to the ordained. If only the priest can design the liturgy, then those who aren't ordained are excluded. If only the altar guild can arrange the vestments, then those who are outside of the guild are excluded. If only the trained florist can make the Advent wreath, then people who simply have joy in the beauty of leaves and flowers are excluded. If only "Christian" art is acceptable for the church's use, then whole parts of the world's cultures are excluded. If we only purchase goods from religious supply houses, then amateurs are excluded. Exclusion stops transformation dead in its tracks. What we need are more people involved in making more of the church with more stuff, not fewer people who control the means of the church's production. As my friend Nadia Bolz-Weber says of her congregation, House for All Sinners and Saints, "We're anti-excellence and pro-participation." We have to use everything that we can to make church together, not just what a group considers "perfect" for the church's use.

Perfectionism is the enemy of transformation. The church doesn't need more people pushing the perfectionism agenda;

it needs more love for the process of creation. While we must strive in the creative process, we can't make striving for perfection the main point of what we are doing. Otherwise, we are just imitating the machinery of the world where the weak and imperfect are marginalized, and the "flawless" and powerful are put at the center. What the church needs are more opportunities for people to sit together and simply make things. "When two or three are gathered" includes those who gather as makers, and Christ's Spirit will be in their midst, even when what they make is homemade. Especially when what they make is homemade. God's Commonwealth is about concrete action. It is more than having the right opinions or the right ideas. It is all about living in relationships that are creative and generative, trusting that God is continuing creation in the process. God's Commonwealth isn't designed for privilege or perfection; it is for the whole Community of the New Covenant. The only requirement is desire. Everyone has a part to play in making church.

Making church is always done in companionship with others. Sharing work is a transformative experience. Brian comments on his participation: "People appreciated what I was doing with my hands, helping set this up for Easter or whatever, but then I started realizing that it was more than volunteering for volunteer sake, it's also just being present." Being present in the community with others, engaging in creative work, opens us to new opportunities for growth and change. The work of making church happen is not just about accomplishing tasks; the greater benefit is being together with the other members of the community, sharing not only the work but also the experience of creating something for the sake of the whole congregation. Not only is this dynamic at work when we're creating a beautiful space for worship; we are strengthened by doing functional work like cleaning the kitchen or pulling weeds in the garden. Sharing work nurtures and enriches the life of the congregation. What congregations must provide are opportunities to share work freely. This is where transformation happens.

As the rector of the church, learning to share work has been liberating for me. It has also required me to understand the congregation and myself in a new way. I was formed as a priest believing that I had privileges and responsibilities that nobody else could touch. Almost none of them were my canonical duties; most were only the turf that I was taught to guard carefully. St. Gregory's strives to live out one of our core values of liturgy in the ways we make church together: we give work away. A visitor who comes to worship with us will see many people active in the service. Members make the vestments and arrange the worship space, light the lamps and candles, proclaim the Scriptures, serve communion, speak their prayers aloud, make coffee, and clean up when it is time to go home.

Congregation members make church week after week; this is how we proclaim that our relationships are rooted in the worship and praise of God. We place a premium on giving work away so that each person can share in the work of making church. Making church means letting people do things not because they have to, but because they are free to do so. What I have discovered in sharing my authority with the members of St. Gregory's is that my work as a priest is enriched. I am free to give away my work in ways that amplify what God is doing in our midst. As a result, the congregation is filled with people of all ages and stages of life that are competent leaders. All of this is a perfect definition of the word liturgy: work done by a few for the sake of everyone else.

Welcoming the Stranger: Seeing God through Other Eyes

*Here's this new thing and we'll
find a way to make it part of our
shared duty. We'll find a way.*

—*Mark L.*

G OD SENDS STRANGERS into the church to mess things up. Strangers don't mean to do this; it's just the way that social systems operate. Strangers come into a known social gathering, one that has learned over time how to operate, what norms are agreeable, and what its relationships mean. Strangers come into these systems more or less ignorant of the way things have always operated in churches. Today, there is no single set of cultural norms related to church that everyone shares. There is no canon of behavior for going to church. If there are norms of behavior in a local congregation, they are less and less understood by first-time church visitors. For some, this is bad news; for others, it is very good news. Strangers come into a social system that insiders understand, and their very presence makes that understanding open to debate. God sends strangers to open the church to a new understanding of its identity. Despite a congregation's best efforts at keeping things the same, strangers bring the disruptive presence of the Spirit with them into the assembly.

Early in my ordained ministry, I was a Canon at Christ Church Cathedral in Houston, Texas. Christ Church is a congregation that has enlivened the heart of that city since 1839. It has outreach programs to aid the homeless, as well as a brilliant liturgy and an exquisite music program. To step into Christ Church is to step into a world where it seems that peace and beauty have always been the order of the day—until it's not. I remember a perfect Sunday morning at Christ Church Cathedral. The sun shone through the stained glass windows, and I stood in the pulpit, preaching the love of God. As I recall, I was talking about Christian responsibility to those in need. I preached from the arrogance and privilege of a newly minted priest. And then it happened. God sent a stranger into our midst. And we all witnessed the coming of Christ.

I didn't know his name; I'd never seen him before. But I knew his type. He was dirty, crazy-eyed, homeless. He was one of the thousands of men who walk the streets and sidewalks and alleys of every American city, muttering angrily under their breath. The people in authority over the cathedral always tried to manage homeless men when they came inside. Not that we would exclude them, the cathedral was a place for everyone. But when a homeless person would walk in, vaguely breathing some threat, the ushers would keep an eye on him.

On this perfect Sunday morning, the homeless stranger walked into the church and quickly up the central aisle, bypassing the ushers and heading straight to the front pew, maybe ten feet in front of the pulpit where I stood. He came to the pew where a friend of mine customarily sat with her family. And he did look dangerously unstable, dangerously unpredictable. He seemed unwilling to be managed by the religious niceties that everyone else either consciously or unconsciously embraced. He waved his hand at my friend, indicating that she had somehow mistakenly taken his regular seat. She moved down the pew a space and let him sit down. An usher, having missed his chance to corral him safely in the back of the cathedral, hurried up the central aisle after him, squatting next to where the man sat. I watched and preached from the high pulpit. God has a wicked sense of humor. When the homeless stranger walked in that morning, I had just hit on the main theme of my sermon: the Christian responsibility to treat homeless people with respect. I did not expect that the invitation to disruption would be taken so literally by God.

I stood, and I preached. Then I looked. And the homeless stranger was crying. His face was wet with tears. Then I looked again. And my friend had wrapped her smooth, manicured hand around his, comforting him as I had seen her comfort her children. At the Peace, I went to my friend and asked, "Is everything okay?" She replied, "Everything is perfect." At communion, she walked hand in hand with her homeless brother to the altar, and I placed the bread of life into his hurt hands. And then he was gone. Like the angel at the empty tomb, his message was given, and he disappeared.

Despite our best efforts, the social system in most congregations will seek to carefully separate people into "us" and "them." We do this because we are afraid. We carry a fear through the church like a wet sofa, fear weighing us down, exhausting us on the way that leads to eternal life. We fear the lack of control that is the very hallmark of Jesus's pathway. We fear the strangeness of the gospel's obvious exhortation: "It is not the healthy who need a doctor, but the sick. I have not come to call the righteous, but sinners." But our fear will not stop the Good News. And this is the Good News: we get to live for the sake of the world, as God truly knows it to be, not just the way we fear it might be. We get to risk embracing strangers with the same embrace God gives. We get to build our future on God's promise to come to us in the presence of the stranger. We get to have the church broken by strangers.

Strangers break open the church and give everyone inside a new experience of God's beauty. Beauty is not only a gift *from* God; it is an experience of God. Beauty is the glory of God, not only a way that we talk about God's glory. Whenever and wherever God is present, there is beauty—including in the presence of strangers. The congregation's work is to welcome strangers with the same wondering desire as we welcome the coming of God's beauty in our midst. But more than that, our responsibility is to welcome the opportunity of transformation that comes in the presence of strangers. In welcoming the stranger, we must expect that we will be remade as a community and as individuals. Welcoming the stranger into our lives must be filled with generosity and void of judgment. We make this choice to welcome strangers because we want to see more of what God is doing in the world and the church.

Since our founding, St. Gregory's has made a preferential choice to welcome strangers into the liturgy without an expectation that they will conform themselves to the congregation's faith or understanding. This insight is based on one of the primary assumptions of our common life: God, who longs to draw the whole world in love, is revealed to the community in the presence of the stranger. Each Sunday we begin our liturgy with this prayer: "Blessed be God the Word, who came to his own and his own received him not; for in this way God glorifies the stranger. O God, show us your image in all who come to us today that we may welcome them and you." Show us! Give to us! We are like the little children that Jesus insists we must become if we are to inherit the Kingdom of God: we want what we want now! We want to see more of God, more of God's action in the world, and we believe that strangers are the ones who are uniquely able to show God to us.

It is God who glorifies strangers, and God's people respond to this divine action by doing the same thing. Glorifying the stranger admits that he or she brings a gift to us: newness, possibility, and potential. This is what makes the stranger beautiful to us. When a stranger comes into the assembly, it is a sign of God's presence, making the whole world new. In response, we go out of our way to welcome them, hoping that, in the encounter, we will discover something that we had not known before about God and God's action in the world. Randy says, "I can share myself and whatever joy I have with strangers." Sharing ourselves with strangers begins in our desire to become a friend to the stranger, to know and be known by the stranger. We do this in the context of the liturgy, and we can carry on this practice in our lives outside of the church. Our hope of becoming a friend with another person is beautiful; it is the moment when the stranger ceases being a threat and is revealed as bearing God's image.

Whether or not congregations choose to welcome strangers is the critical question of the day. Until the church understands itself to be peripheral, strange, and outside the dominance culture, it won't be interested in bringing strangers into the center of its life. Perhaps the question for congregations is, "Can we leave our egocentrism and see where God is emerging right now—even if it is strange to us?" The way the church answers this question carries the hope of transforming the world. One of the unique gifts that the church bears for the world is our ability to welcome strangers, as they are. We cannot welcome strangers on the basis of their conformity to our practice. We must welcome them as a sign of God's presence with us, showing us what God is doing in the world, breaking us open to see more of God. Sometimes, we must ourselves become strangers in order to see the work of God in the world.

⚜

On All Souls' Day 2011, I went across the bay to Oakland with my friend Sara and her wife Martha to witness the general strike called by the Occupy Oakland organizers. Thousands gathered in downtown Oakland to march in the streets, learn about corporate injustice, protest economic inequality, and simply stand in prayerful solidarity. There were many things that I saw and felt and heard and smelled that were overwhelmingly beautiful. I was blessed by a little girl who held a bundle of smoking sage before me, making the sign of the cross with it. I was delighted by the blazing energy of the young queer kids who launched into an impromptu flag routine in the middle of the march. I wore my black shirt and clerical collar—I figured that I didn't have to carry a sign if I dressed up like a priest. People stopped me and asked if they could take my picture, sort of like seeing an exotically dressed native on a foreign vacation. There was clearly an orthodoxy to the Occupy demonstration, an orthodoxy that my clergy garb sometimes offended. In the midst of one of the largest protests on the west coast, I was a stranger.

I am not much of a protester. I seldom attend marches or rallies. I went to the Occupy protest to be a visual sign of an institution that many there understood to be the enemy. We began the march, slowly, from downtown toward Lake Merritt. I wore my dark glasses and a solemn expression. "You look like the Terminator," Martha said. I tried smiling. We passed by the Roman Catholic Cathedral of Christ the Light. I saw that someone had spray painted "NO GODS AND NO MASTERS" on the wall of the church. "Stupid anarchists," I thought. As we marched along the edge of Lake Merritt, I heard a loud pop and saw someone break a window at the Bank of America. Sara saw a small clutch of young men yelling and police nearby and ran toward them. Sara always runs toward trouble. A man on a bicycle pulled up by me and asked me what I thought about it all. I don't know if he asked me because I was dressed like a priest, or because I looked like the Terminator, or because I am light skinned and he was dark skinned. We had a reasonable conversation ranging from the ideal of peaceful demonstration to the problem of the Electoral College. In the midst of what felt like chaos and dread, two strangers were trying to understand what was happening. This is the point of protesting: to gather with friends and strangers, in the midst of confusion, and try and understand what is happening. Admitting that I was a stranger opened me to the fact that I needed the intelligence of someone else, someone unlike me, to understand what in the world was happening.

As followers of Jesus Christ, we are strangers in the world. Being a stranger can be overwhelming. Finding yourself a stranger in the world can make you long nostalgically for the way things were, particularly if you are the sort of person whom the past privileged. Like the Hebrews in the wilderness, we may long for the fleshpots of our captivity. We may want things just to calm down, and return to "normal." One Sunday, after a particularly acrimonious conversation with a parishioner, I was slumped over in the sacristy trying to get it together for the next service. Margaret walked in and asked me if I was okay. I said, "Sometimes I just long for the church of the 1950s where everyone did what the rector said." She put her hand on my shoulder and gently replied, "I know. But you'd have been miserable back then."

We cannot return to the past. We cannot go back to a time and place where everyone knew how to behave in church, where people conformed to church ways to be a part of the church. That world has passed away—thanks be to God. As we continue to grow into post-Christendom, as we learn new ways of being the church, we get to embrace our identity as strangers. We get to embrace the truth prophetically uttered by Flannery O'Connor: "You shall know the truth, and the truth shall make you odd."

The tendency of human culture is to work hard at creating a world where nothing changes, and if that doesn't work to turn to more violent means of suppression. We who follow the way of Jesus Christ have other options. Instead of violence, we have received a particular intelligence. We are to be like the one the gospel tells us is guarding a house: we have to stay alert, stay awake, and keep patience. We must stay awake to our true identity: we are God's beloved. As God's beloved, we are knit together out of God's desire for us. That is our identity. We are made as God's beloved, the apple of God's eye, and the object of God's desire. This is the identity that we share with every other stranger we encounter. We are, all of us, God's beloved.

※

By welcoming strangers, and by embracing our own strangeness, we learn more about our own desire to be new, to understand more about God's presence in the world and how we are transformed by it. Randy describes it like this: "I think that we're dancing through history and that we live out the idea of welcoming the stranger. That daily and weekly, that's before us: welcoming the stranger to become God's friend." People at St. Gregory's welcome the stranger, not only as an attempt at social inclusion but to know God. Welcoming the stranger is not just about etiquette; it is a theological and spiritual exercise that expects the beauty of holiness to be revealed in the lives of strangers as God glorifies them.

Mark lives near the Haight-Ashbury neighborhood in San Francisco. Although it was ground zero for the Summer of Love fifty years ago, the neighborhood now swings from being touristy to a layover for homeless people. Like so many of our neighborhoods, it has experienced both the highs and lows of gentrification. Not long ago, the old neighborhood grocery store was turned into a Whole Foods Market. Now it's shared by hipster parents shopping for organic food and homeless men hunting for their next fix. Mark shops there. He told me a story about how he sees God glorifying the stranger at Whole Foods: "For the last six months or so I've realized that there's a particular man. He's very down-and-out. He lives in a sort of group home. He's an older man in a wheelchair that I run into more often than seems to be coincidence. When that started to happen, instead of just sort of thinking, 'Isn't that odd,' I had a different attitude with myself, which was, 'God is putting this man in my path in some way. And I want to engage in that.' And so, whenever I see him, we sit and we talk. I make sure he's had some food that day. Yesterday we had a long talk about his background, and he was telling me how cold he is at night. So the next time I see him, I can give him some blankets."

There is a beguiling social contract that tries to separate Mark from the down-and-out man at Whole Foods. It is the kind of social contract that allows me to look away the instant I might catch a stranger's eye. We get used to this agreement that we make with the stranger and ourselves, to the degree that the stranger stops being a person and becomes a problem. When we dehumanize strangers, we don't have to deal with them, let alone love them. But when our imagination is transformed, when we begin to look at strangers as those who are a part of ourselves, we cannot look away. If we do look away, our consciences remind us that we have been changed. Once you begin to look at the stranger as beautiful, you cannot see them otherwise without diminishing yourself. Mark found that there was a divine intention in a seemingly random encounter with a stranger. Rather than ignore this calling, he chose to pursue it and engage a stranger in conversation, discovering that the neediness of the other was something that he could address himself. Mark saw the man at Whole Foods and was changed by what he saw. His small act of social engagement became an opportunity for transformation. And in all of this he witnessed the magnificence of God who glorifies the stranger.

We glorify the stranger because God glorifies the stranger. To "glorify" means to reveal the essence of a thing. God glorifies the stranger so that we can understand the essential truth of our humanity, that God's love for everyone is the only thing that has the power to relate us to the other. When God glorifies the stranger, we discover our true identity and our vocation in life. We must glorify the stranger as God does. We do this in the ways that we choose to engage those who are strange to us. Looking at the stranger not as a threat, but as a member of God's household, reveals our mutual identity as God's children. As we pay attention to this identity, we learn to know more of God as revealed in Jesus Christ. That learning isn't an intellectual exercise; it is about love.

Jesus is glorified as he is lifted high upon the cross, drawing all people into his embrace. This is the one thing that he can do to reveal perfectly the essence of God. On the hard wood of the cross, Jesus glorifies God as the one who is absolute, sacrificial love. Jesus reveals what God's love is like by saying, "Look, I'm dying for you—and I'm doing it freely and in full control of the situation. Don't worry about how you will know me— I've known you perfectly by becoming perfectly like you—even bleeding and dying like you." This is God's love in action. God joins in solidarity with us, showing the fullness of love. There is no place that God has not gone before us because Jesus has revealed God to us perfectly. So, when Jesus weeps, God weeps. When Jesus bleeds, God bleeds. When Jesus dies, God dies. When Jesus rises to new life, God promises to rise up in us anew.

Jesus gives us a way to become visible to the world around us. For the world to be able to see him, Jesus gives his followers a new commandment: "Love one another." The promise is that whenever we love, the world will see what Jesus is like and if the world sees what Jesus is like, then the world will see what God is like. Not because we are perfect, but because we were first loved into life by God. Everyone will be able to see God because God first loved us. As we enact the love God gives us, we are glorified, and we glorify the stranger.

�֍

The gospel begins with hunger. All of the feeding stories in the gospel point us toward our hunger, as well as our Eucharistic fellowship. You can't separate our spiritual hunger from God's desire to fill us with God's grace. Our spiritual hunger isn't an accident, not something with which we, unfortunately, have to live. Our hunger is the proper human response to God's promise to fill us. Although Jesus could have chosen any number of ways to signify God's grace, he chose a meal. But it's not just any meal. It is a meal where everyone is welcome. It is a meal in which the spiritual hunger of the world is met by the love of God in Jesus Christ. From the thousands who gathered on hillsides and grassy meadows, to the few who gathered to eat that last night before he was glorified, to those who gather in our churches Sunday by Sunday, Jesus welcomes everyone to his table.

Jesus chose to dine with the unready as well as the ready, the pure with the impure, because he first seeks our hunger. Jesus chose to demonstrate his Abba's Commonwealth of peace by tossing the regulations about who could dine with whom right out the dining room window. As the prophet Isaiah before him, he enacted a banquet prepared for all people and called it the cornerstone of the new community he formed out of his flesh.

Jesus doesn't blame people for their hunger; he doesn't punish them for being hungry. He doesn't charge the crowds a fee for their meal. He doesn't set up a velvet rope to keep some from the table until they are worthy enough to dine. He doesn't quiz them to see if they understand how to eat with him. The only response that Jesus makes to the hungry multitudes is to have compassion on them and feed them. This is why the church has to do the same: to welcome the spiritually hungry with spiritual food for them to eat.

In the account of his illegal seminary in Nazi Germany, *Life Together*, Dietrich Bonhoeffer writes, "The table fellowship of Christians implies obligation. It is our daily bread that we eat, not my own. We share our bread. Thus, we are firmly bound to one another not only in the Spirit but also in our whole physical being. The one bread that is given to our fellowship links us together in a firm covenant."[13] The food that Jesus gives to the hungry crowd is food that belongs to all people—the unclean with the pure of heart, the prepared with the novice, all we undeserving and infinitely beloved. His disciples don't seem to get this at first. In the Gospel of Mark's story of the thousands being fed, they see the great hunger of the crowd and belief in their scarcity more than God's abundance. The best idea they come up with is exclusion: "Send them away so that they may go into the surrounding country and villages and buy something for themselves to eat" (Mark 6:36). The disciples expect that the crowd should do what they ought to do by the crushing standards of the world—feed themselves.

We in the church are too often like Jesus's disciples. The disciples are ready to send the crowds away because they're afraid of being overwhelmed by hunger. There just isn't enough, as far as the disciples can see. Jesus sees something more. By his words and action, Jesus tells the disciples that they don't have

---

13 Dietrich Bonhoeffer and John W. Doberstein, *Life Together: The Classic Exploration of Christian Community* (New York: Harper & Row, 1989), 68.

to rely on their resources to do what's needed. The truth is that God will give everyone—strangers and friends—what's needed to do God's will. We simply have to live as if the foundational model of the universe is found in Jesus feeding people. The only thing that can stop the hungry being fed is our inactivity. When we fail to feed the hungry, when we fail to welcome everyone to our table-fellowship, we are obliged to repent and return to God. The key to our return is our own memory of hunger. So, remember a time when you were hungry. Remember a time when you were excluded from the table. Remember a time when you could not get the food that you needed. In other words, turn to empathy. Return to the ache in your belly and in your soul. Hunger will instruct you in the way to return to God. It is only when we identify with the hungry that we are ready to fulfill our spiritual obligation to welcome strangers to our table.

St. Gregory's is well known for our long-standing custom of open communion: giving the bread and wine which are Christ's Body and Blood to everyone, regardless of their having been baptized or not. Almost every member of St. Gregory's identifies this practice as contributing to their transformation. We don't just talk about eucharistic theology; we enact it every Sunday in this very deliberate way. Mark L. says, "People come in and cry the first time they are communicated, and their life is fundamentally changed. And I'm part of a congregation that gives God that kind of elbow room." We expect God to be God and to act in the course of the liturgy. Mark L. continues, "I can see how eating with anybody says something about what God is like: that God just gives himself, herself, to everybody, whether you like it or not—and that I can do the same. I can give myself to people, not push myself: I can give myself freely to people." In the same way that God gives freely to all people, we are empowered to give ourselves to people in service. We get to act as God does in generously giving whatever we can for the sake of healing and wholeness in the world. Freely sharing communion with everyone has the power to transform lives, and to do so in a way that has theological integrity and meaning, based on Christ's commandment of love.

Love is the essence of the Eucharist. We show our love by welcoming all people to come and join us: those who are prepared and those who are unprepared, those who have walked long with Jesus and those who have been a long time away from Jesus, those who are full of faith and those whose faith is small. We invite all people to come and share, just as we have been called to share. The Eucharist is a love feast, a mutual sharing of what we have for the sake of the entire world. It is the way in which we show our belief that the new life of the resurrection is for all people, that all people are invited to come and live.

People worry about the practice of open communion. Some are convinced that there are unworthy people who mustn't come to the table and receive. Or, there are people who consider themselves unworthy to receive. When we have a wedding or a funeral, times when there are many more visitors than usual, I see this. I give communion by walking through the standing crowd in the rotunda, handing out bread while someone follows with a chalice of wine. Sometimes people look at me and just shake their heads "no." I worry about this. I worry that there have been times when someone convinced these folks that they were not worthy to come and share what Jesus gives. That someone has said, in so many words, "you are not welcome here." As if there were some way that one could find worth outside of God's invitation to come and receive.

The greatest threat to the Eucharist is not deficient theology or a lack of understanding. The greatest threat to the Eucharist is that we do not show our love. When we do not live out of love, we place a huge question mark over the meaning of the Eucharist. The Body of Christ is not just a term to reference the church. The Body of Christ is every person who is deprived of dignity, or freedom, or life. Love isn't optional. The Eucharist is contingent on the way we show our love. Love dares to act for the sake of justice and reconciliation. Love feeds the hungry and serves the sick and frees the imprisoned. Real presence means God giving life to the whole world: abundantly, lavishly, and freely.

✄

To be transformed in its shared life, congregations have to welcome everyone into the community irrespective of belief, differences, or familiarity. Welcoming strangers, without requiring them to know everything about our congregational culture, is transformative. It's this kind of generous welcome that places the experience of the stranger at the center of the community's imagination. Designing the liturgy, formation, community life, and service in ways that speak clearly to strangers is something that any congregation in the Episcopal Church can do. The congregation's need for welcoming strangers must be expressed as part of its own culture and practice.

St. Gregory's exists as a community to demonstrate, in all that we do, the day when God will be all in all. To this end we seek to structure our shared life to show that God is reaching out to all beings, calling everyone into friendship. There can be no distinctions; God has already established all of us as beloved friends. As God's friends, we are being made new. In Paul's Epistle to the Colossians the writer says, "You have stripped off the old self with its practices and have clothed yourselves with the new self, which is being renewed in knowledge according to the image of its creator. In that renewal there is no longer Greek and Jew, circumcised and uncircumcised, barbarian, Scythian, slave and free; but Christ is all and in all" (Colossians 3:9b–11). God in Christ is making the church anew, breaking down divisions, and calling us to renewal of life. Our renewal as God's people means that we cannot define ourselves against those who are strangers. We are called to see Christ in all people, living in God's friendship.

God is at work breaking down the divisions that deform our

relationships. God is at work in what is strange to us and in us. We must engage the unknown world where God is to be found. We are transformed whenever we recognize God's presence in our experiences, relationships, and efforts at creating what has not yet been known. In all of this, we strive to grow into the image of the Creator, to whom no one is a stranger. Friendship with God, established by the loving service of Jesus Christ to all humanity, remakes the church's identity as a community of friends, each striving to do the work of Christ in the world.

chapter

8

Conclusion: What Do You Want to Become?

Once there was a time when the whole
rational creation formed a single dancing
chorus looking upward to the one leader
of this dance. And the harmony of
motion that they learned from his law
found its way into their dancing.

—*Gregory of Nyssa*

HE HARMONY OF motion. I was thinking about this the Friday before the beginning of Holy Week, sitting in the church. As happens every Friday, the Food Pantry had begun handing groceries to the four hundred hungry people who came to be fed. The church was full of produce: oranges, cabbages, green apples, red potatoes, yogurt, canned and dry goods. The doors had already opened, and the first people had arrived. The ones who come early are predominately Chinese elders who do their part in providing for their extended families, coming to the pantry and other feeding stations in the city to get groceries.

This Friday was different from many; at the end of the building opposite the piles of groceries and circling lines of people who had come for food was a quintet of men, rehearsing for a Holy Week concert, singing Thomas Tallis's *Lamentations of Jeremiah.* They stood in the apse of the church and sang the sad, stately music that begs the people to return to God: "Jerusalem, Jerusalem, return unto the Lord thy God." The sound of the singing mixed with the sound of the pantry clients as they chatted with the volunteers who come, week by week, to do the work of Christ and his people: feeding the hungry, comforting the afflicted, caring for strangers. The singing enfolded the space in a complex, Renaissance harmony as the hungry people walked round and round the altar, receiving the fruit of the earth as freely as the whole human family receives the grace of God. At one end of the building a quintet of men created beauty in the beautiful space, and at the other the volunteers and clients were doing the same thing; the quintet made exquisite music, the pantry made food available for hungry strangers, and each was beautiful. In this mad confluence of the expected and unexpected, transformation was happening, and it was happening because of St. Gregory of Nyssa Episcopal Church.

When I began to write about transformation in people's lives, the first question I had to ask was whether or not people change. I'd hear the cynical voice in my head saying that change just wasn't that likely. Sure, people might want to change parts of their lives, make *superficial* changes, make *decorative* changes—but *deep* change? I just didn't know. But then I started talking to the people in my church about their experiences. Do the things that we do at St. Gregory's change you? Can you tell me about how that happens? The surprising thing was that people did change, and they talked easily about the ways that change—transformation—happened for them. However, this doesn't mean that change is inevitable in every congregation. We need to be honest about our need to strive for transformation. We need to face the systemic forces at play in congregations that work to keep things the same. We need to look at our own desire for change in a world that deeply needs what congregations have to offer. And then we have to act.

Transformation happens because of the kind of everyday events that we share in congregational life. The transformation that I hoped for, the thing that I've staked my work on for decades, did happen. People make personal insights, develop new relationships, take up spiritual practices, and change the ways that they behave. For some of the people at St. Gregory's, the experience of transformation is profound, shaking the foundations of their lives. For others, transformation is something that continues to sneak up on them, moving them to change in subtle ways. It's the things that we always do at St. Gregory's, practices that we can take for granted, that empower transformation. Things like living with beauty at the center of our shared lives. Things like working together to engage our neighbors and strive for justice in our shared lives. Things like living together in friendship, even when, as Margaret says plainly, people annoy the shit out of us.

Transformation isn't a phenomenon unique to St. Gregory's; any church can work for the sake of people's transformation. The first thing that a congregation must do is live out of its hope in the power of God to transform people's lives. The congregation's ministries must be an expression of the effervescent and eternal life of Jesus Christ, setting the world ablaze. In this light, everyone is welcome into the love of God that will not stop until all things are made new. Our first job is to step out of the center, recognizing God's work in the world, and to take our part in it, not trying to force God into the work that we're already doing. In order to take part in God's work, congregations must keep their gaze fixed on the servant nature of Christ and his sacrificial love for all beings. Congregations cannot work for the transformation of people's lives from a place of arrogance or privilege. It is only with humility and joy that there is power to work for transformation. And the question that congregations must continue to ask is simple and challenging: What do you want to become?

This becoming begins with beauty. People are transformed by the encounter with beauty. People change when they encounter beauty not just in physical objects, but also in the stranger, in the unknown other. This encounter creates the opportunity for people to experience the presence of God. This experience has the power to open new insight, something that is critical in the process of transformation. What constitutes beauty in the congregation is complex; beauty must address the issues of taste, culture, and economics. All of these factors complicate the approach of beauty. So we begin our approach from a different place: we must approach beauty as we approach God. Whenever there is liveliness, openness, and authenticity, there is beauty and there is God. Whenever truth, harmony, and fairness are shared together, there is beauty and there is God. Beauty captures our imagination and directs it toward God. This is the beauty that can feed the hungry souls of those who come to be made new by God's presence.

God is always with us. However, our awareness of God is intensified when we come together for worship. At St. Gregory's, we have found that the liturgy is the best place for forming our identity as a community. Worship is a container for mystery and a field upon which mystery plays. Worship assures us that the mystery of God is present and active in our midst. A congregation's worship must work to show that God is powerfully present, with promises of love, calling us to return to our true selves. Worship must be about discipleship, the whole congregation working together to be formed into the image of God. This must include insiders and outsiders, adults and children, experts and amateurs. Otherwise, worship is too easily molded to the values and norms of the domination culture that surrounds us. The congregation's worship must be attuned to what is marginal; we must step out of the center for this to work.

The congregation's liturgy must be designed for those who have never worshiped with us before, who are just outside our doors looking in to see if they are welcome. Whenever strangers come to worship with us, we have to turn out from ourselves and toward those we don't yet know with genuine hospitality. This is more than an exercise in etiquette for the congregation; it is an enacted theology of God's Commonwealth. When we welcome the stranger into our liturgy, we are provided with the opportunity to learn about our desire to be made new. When strangers come to worship with us, they bring the gift of a new appreciation of God, and we come to experience God's presence more richly. Worship empowers us to reach out to strangers, to dare to engage them as partners in God's work in the world. This encounter brings transformation. Even hearing about another person's grace-filled encounter with a stranger inspires transformation. When the congregation reaches out to the stranger, seeking to put them at the center of our life, it is not out of a sense of guilt. Instead, we turn to the stranger with generosity, love, and hospitality. We are empowered by our desire to know more about God. When we reach out to strangers, we will see more of God at work in the world.

Worship will form the identity of the congregation. We discover our true identity from eating together at the altar. As we freely receive the bread and wine, we not only think about our identity, we experience ourselves as God's friends. The experience of living in friendship with God is not confined to congregational insiders; everyone is invited to experience friendship with God through the loving service of Christ. God's friendship comes freely to everyone; it is an expression of the eternal love that is God the Holy Trinity. Friendship with God, the initiative that God makes in binding the Church in one, comes with the expectation that we will be transformed. God's love is freely poured out for us so that we can share it with all beings forging new friendships with those we encounter both inside and outside the congregation. All of these relationships—with God, with friends, and with strangers—work to transform us, both individually and as a community. In forging relationships of love, based on God's invitation to friendship, the congregation can make a rule of life, a way to grow in maturity and depth.

Every time that the congregation assembles in worship, service, friendship or work, God is present. The coming of God, sometimes startling, sometimes unexpected, is always beautiful. God's beauty will come in ways that we hadn't imagined, in the lives of strangers, for example. This is why, to see the fullness of God's beauty, congregations must be open to receive the beauty of God from everyone who comes through the doors. Beauty and the presence of God can't be divided. Too often we stop the approach of beauty because of our fears: of scarcity, of conflict, or of shame. But beauty keeps coming; God keeps unbolting the doors to our hearts and coming in. Beauty is reckless and profligate; it always seeks to draw human desire to itself. The wildness of beauty may seem beyond the ken of the church, but God wants to be seen in wild places. Everyone who comes to church brings beauty. If the church wants to see more of God, we have to gratefully receive beauty, celebrate it, and draw life from it. The approach of beauty in the church brings transformation.

God's work in the world is always about restoring what has been broken by injustice and oppression to relationships of love. Congregations cannot engage the community they serve as a kind of social work apart from the strong love of God. When we take up God's work in the world, we need to do so relationally, striving to build new friendships with those who are victims of injustice and oppression. When we do this work together, strangers become friends, and their experiences influence our lives. The one thing that stops this dynamic is when we consider our justice work as an obligation or a form of service to the "less fortunate." This renders the unknown other as little more than a project or a problem to be solved. But when congregations recognize that we all share in a single humanity, when we see the other as a friend of God, we can enter into a spirit of service that is continuous with the Spirit of Jesus. Because of this, congregations are strengthened, as are the communities outside our walls. All of this is about creating a spiritual community and not operating a social service agency. The way we share work is beautiful. In this, we are transformed.

The divisions that separate social groups, the economic and class divides that feed a terror of the other, the perceived scarcity of goods and exploitation of the weak are all concerns of the congregation. Each of these concerns and all that are to come in human history are first spiritual and personal crises. This is another reason why congregations must take up the work of social engagement relationally. Social engagement is a spiritual practice. As with any spiritual practice, the goal of social engagement is transformation, both of the one being served and the one doing the service. The energy required to address the crises of the coming days is the same energy that flows from the Eucharist; what is common is offered to God and transformed into heavenly food. The Eucharist is the template of the congregation's social engagement; the way that we share communion will directly influence the way we serve in the community. Congregations must serve others in the Spirit of Christ. We must welcome the other person—friend or stranger—as holy.

When we come to see the stranger as something besides a threat, when we see that person as a friend of God, we are changed. Friendship works to transform us when it is inclusive of others unlike us. Friendship in the congregation cannot be from personal affinity alone. Friendship in the congregation is always a reflection of the friendship that God extends to us. When we approach strangers from this perspective, congregations will discover that crossing social boundaries is transformative. Then, the congregation becomes a place where people's understanding of the world and themselves is increased.

Friendship in congregational life is not identical with friendship found in other social groups. The friendship into which God invites us is based on mutual service, striving for the good of the other, and including strangers as members of the household of God. The love that is expressed in our friendship is *agape*, love that commits persons to one another selflessly. This is the love that Christ commands the church to practice as the basis of its common life: it is gospel love. Without gospel love, congregations lose the distinctive vocation to form a kinship network that welcomes all people as members, brothers, and sisters. Neither age, gender, role, class nor any other social category can be used to distinguish between friends in the church; all must be welcome in the household of God.

Friendship in the congregation doesn't depend on our personal feelings. Our life in friendship is formed by God's choice. God calls everyone into friendship. This is crucial to our future. The church is the last truly public institution in North American culture. Everyone can come to church as they are, on their own terms, without having to pay an entrance fee. The public nature of the church makes it both precious, and potentially unmanageable. But when we choose management of people over welcoming people, we fail to live out the friendship of God. Friendship in the congregation is based on God's free choice to love all people. As friendship is practiced in the church, welcoming relationships with those who are similar and dissimilar, our life is deepened, and our mission is clarified. There can be no strangers in the church. Friendship welcomes transformation in the church.

All of which means that we must welcome everyone irrespective of their beliefs, differences, or familiarity. At St. Gregory's, this generous welcome of strangers is most clearly seen as the bread and wine of the Eucharist are given freely to all people. As Christ chose to dine in ways that scandalized his contemporaries, so must his Body, the Church, become a scandal by including all people at the Eucharistic table. The free welcome, extended by God's people, empowers transformation in our lives. Welcoming strangers, without requiring them to conform to the established culture of the church, is a transformative experience for us. This generous welcome places the experience of a first-time visitor at the center of the church's life. This is the kind of welcome that will transform the church.

The congregation is called to find Christ in all people. By mixing the expected and the unexpected, the church gains a sense that God is at work breaking down the divisions that deform human beings. When the expected and the unexpected are mixed together, our attention is captured, and we become focused on the point of God's engagement with humankind: the intermingling that we had thought was unclean is revealed to be the purpose of God. At the beginning of creation, God called all that was made good; it is only in our blindness to God's great love for humankind that we make what is good into what is impure. God's ongoing engagement with us is a way of revealing that the goodness and holiness of creation continue to transform. St. Gregory's concern for beauty, harmony, friendship, engagement, and fairness is a response to God's wooing of humankind. Our work seeks to point out the places where God is coming with promises of love.

In all aspects of our common life, St. Gregory's expects that the people who come to share in its fellowship will be transformed. St. Gregory's is not just a place to seek comfort; it is a place in which everyone can turn from one way of being to a new way of becoming. In other words, it is a community that calls people to repent. But it is not the image of the street preacher ranting to the crowds that we advocate. Rather, it is the image of a welcoming God, who rushes toward us with arms spread wide and offers each more than can be imagined. When we come together with others in need of repentance—both old friends and strangers, children and adults, turning toward God—we are remade. This is entirely based on our desire to be new.

Instead of building on a foundation of guilt and inadequacy, congregations must build on the assumption that God desires relationship with everyone and delights in our striving to be made new. Congregations don't have to identify the other person's faults and seek to change them. We are bound together in relationships established by God. We are all God's beloved children who stand in the assurance of God's love. The harmony of the motion of beauty, penetrating the goal of justice, bound in the bonds of friendship, attunes us to transformation. Congregations will be changed in this dance. New opportunities for knowing God, and expressing God's wisdom, will come to us. God will be revealed anew to the entire congregation. We will find that we have more love to give than can be imagined.

I have learned that the value of congregational life is not diminished as we live in the twenty-first century. Although discouragement is always a part of leadership in the church, it is never the last word. God is continually making everything new, including the congregation and its leaders. In beauty, justice, and friendship, congregations must strive to do the work that makes us free: to be made anew in our common life. Congregations exist for those who have not yet come through the doors of our buildings. God established every congregation for strangers and seekers, for the prepared and the unprepared, for the righteous and the impure. It is my hope that, as the years progress, congregations will continue to be places that welcome those who are hungry, who seek to be fed in body and soul. It is my hope that all who come will discover within the congregation's walls a place that says "yes" more than it says "no." It is my hope that congregations will always be places where God is seen in the common and extraordinary things of life.